What God Desires

What God Desires

Matthew 25: Ministries

THE STORY OF
The Center for Humanitarian Aid and Disaster Relief

Wendell E. Mettey

Providence House Publishers
WWW.PROVIDENCEHOUSE.COM
FRANKLIN, TENNESSEE

Unless otherwise indicated, scripture quotations are taken from HOLY BIBLE, NEW INTERNATIONAL VERSION®. Copyright © 1973, 1978, 1984 by International Bible Society. Used by permission of Zondervan Publishing House.

Printed in the United States of America

12   11   10   09   08   1   2   3   4   5

Library of Congress Control Number: 2008922353

ISBN: 978-1-57736-410-8

Cover design by LeAnna Massingille

PROVIDENCE HOUSE PUBLISHERS
238 Seaboard Lane • Franklin, Tennessee 37067
www.providencehouse.com
800-321-5692

To Michael Brandy and Dave Knust

and

in memory of June Keeling

Contents

Preface

My purpose in writing *What God Desires* is best expressed in the opening verses of the Gospel of Luke:

> Many have undertaken to draw up an account of the things that have been fulfilled among us, just as they were handed down to us by those who from the first were eyewitnesses and servants of the word. Therefore, since I myself have carefully investigated everything from the beginning, it seemed good also to me to write an orderly account for you . . . (1:1–3).

It also seemed to me that it would be good to write an orderly account of all that had transpired in our attempts to fulfill Matthew 25:34–40:

"For I was hungry and you gave me something to eat, I was thirsty and you gave me
something to drink, I was a stranger and
you invited me in, I needed clothes and
you clothed me, I was sick and you looked
after me, I was in prison and you came to
visit me." Then the righteous will answer
him, "Lord, when did we see you hungry
and feed you, or thirsty and give you something to drink? When did we see you a
stranger and invite you in, or needing
clothes and clothe you? When did we see
you sick or in prison and go to visit you?"
The King will reply, "I tell you the truth,
whatever you did for one of the least of
these brothers of mine, you did for me."

I needed to make known the impact this venture
called Matthew 25: Ministries has had on my life and the
lives of those who have played a vital role in this journey
of faith. I had to express my deepest gratitude to God for
His provision, His sustaining love, the trust He placed in
us, and the front row seats to watch this miraculous story
play out.

As I wrote this story, I asked myself repeatedly, "Why
didn't I keep a journal?" Often the smallest bit of information required the greatest amount of research and time.

I also discovered that my oldest brother, Joe Mettey, is
correct, at least about one thing. As our family genealogist,
he maintains that the most unreliable source of information
is often family stories. Stories are passed orally from one

generation to another with little or no written documentation to corroborate their accuracy.

In writing *What God Desires*, I have diligently searched the Ministries' archives and the Internet for written documentation. However, much to my brother's chagrin, I relied heavily upon the eyewitness testimony of many who were present for the events that took place, including myself. A date may be off by a day or two, or a name misspelled, but I want to assure the reader that I have done extensive research and have endeavored "to draw up an account of the things that have been fulfilled among us" (Luke 1:1). I believe this is a remarkable story, and I hope it inspires readers in their belief in the faithfulness of God.

Lastly, *What God Desires* is a continuation of my first book, *Are Not My People Worthy?*, which tells how it all began, why we took the name Matthew 25: Ministries, and of the struggles, difficulties, blessings, and successes we've had over the years. It tells of our unsuccessful efforts to find a home of our own—a warehouse worthy of our Great God and the poor He calls us to serve. *What God Desires* picks up where *Are Not My People Worthy?* leaves off. In just a couple of years, something truly wonderful took place. Like the mythological phoenix which rose from its own ashes, we were given a place where desirability was hidden by the ashes of years of neglect. This is the story of the Center for Humanitarian Aid and Disaster Relief.

As the hymn writer proclaims, "To God be the glory, great things He has done."

Our twenty-four-foot truck is picking up supplies daily in a one-hundred-mile radius of Cincinnati. Corporations are now donating to us over five million pounds of supplies a year. The staff is growing and volunteers are increasing. We are booking volunteer groups three to four weeks ahead. Each day is a new discovery, challenge, and blessing. Every bill is paid on time—close, but never late. Facing another lease issue and the possibility of another move, my prayers are still for a home of our own. One that is large enough to reach even more of the poor in the world and the United States, and paid for so that our quarter of a million dollars yearly rent payment can go to sending more supplies helping more people. A place I could stand in and say, "Yes, Lord, your people are worthy of this and here it is"!

—Wendell E. Mettey
Are Not My People Worthy?

Chapter One

January 2003: Ten Years Old

When you look at the numbers, 2002 was a very good year. Matthew 25: Ministries shipped out a record number of containers—two hundred and fifty-six forty-foot containers, to be exact. They carried 5,433,183 pounds of high quality, desperately needed humanitarian aid, valued at $37,807,289. Their destination: eighteen impoverished countries around the world and throughout the United States. Here's the breakdown: school supplies, forty containers; clothes, seventy-five containers; fabric for sewing centers, twenty-eight containers; medical supplies and hospital equipment, sixty-six containers; personal care, thirty containers; and thirty-seven miscellaneous containers. The most important number? These supplies impacted the lives of an estimated 1.5 million people.

We also had a good year financially. We managed to pay all of our bills and would begin 2003 with a little financial cushion, or so I thought. When we closed out the 2002 books in mid-January 2003, Chief Financial Officer Don Olson informed me that our little cushion had deflated when he paid the year-ending bills. My brief moment of financial bliss was gone in a nanosecond. Ironically, 2002 was our best year ever financially. It was also, however, our most expensive year. The biggest expense, which waited with its hand out at the first of every month, was our twenty-two-thousand-dollar lease payment. Over two hundred thousand dollars each year was going to landlords instead of the poor. The more successful we became, the larger the warehouse we needed; the larger the warehouse, the greater the expense. Our greatest challenge now was keeping up with our success.

Typically, during the months of November and December we receive between 30 and 35 percent of our yearly income. We were now entering January and February, which were our slowest months. Without that cushion, we were beginning 2003 with only three months of operating income and no savings. The Lord had us on a short financial leash and kept us operating on a pay-as-you-go basis.

After receiving the disappointing news, I stood looking out the window in my study. It was a cold January day. Looking upward at the snow-threatening clouds, I thanked God for seeing us through another year of caring for the poor, those who Jesus called "the least of these." We did not get all that we wanted, but we did receive all that we needed. I also thanked Him for sustaining us for the past ten years. I thought of the numerous not-for-profits that started when we did but had closed up shop, primarily due to the lack of sustainable finances and diminished enthusiasm. Ten years later, we were still open for business. True, we were light on finances, but we were heavy on enthusiasm and strong on commitment. What a ten years they had been for us and the world around us!

During our first ten years, the sixth billionth person was born on Earth. The Shoemaker/Levy comet was torn apart by the tremendous gravitational pull of Jupiter before colliding with the giant planet in July 1994. One piece of the comet impacted Jupiter with the force of six million megatons of TNT—six hundred times the force of all Earth's nuclear arsenal. The impact area of this colossal, seemingly impervious planet was so enormous that several Earths could fit inside it. Suddenly, our little planet seemed a little more vulnerable. Perhaps, I thought with hope, this would bring Earth's inhabitants together in an effort to save humanity when the next cosmic rock came our way, which we were assured would happen.

But if a comet wasn't going to destroy us, there were people who wanted to try. Terrorism raised its ugly head. In February 1993, the first attack on the World Trade Center occurred. A car bomb exploded, killing six people. Completely unaware at the time, this was only the prelude to the many despicable terrorists' attacks to follow. On April 9, 1995, Timothy McVeigh blew up the Murrah Building in Oklahoma City, killing 168 men, women, and children, and injuring hundreds more. We still wonder how a heart could be filled with a hatred strong enough to commit such monstrous acts.

Terrorists were bombing United States' interests abroad, (attacking the *USS Cole* on October 12, 2000, and U.S. embassies in Nairobi, Tanzania, and Kenya on August 7, 1998) but the worst terrorist attack on American soil happened September 11, 2001. Four commercial airliners were hijacked by terrorists who killed many of the crew members. American Airlines flight 11 and United Airlines flight 175 crashed into the World Trade Center Towers, killing thousands; American Airlines flight 77 flew into the Pentagon, and a fourth plane, United Airlines flight 93, crashed in a field in Somerset County, Pennsylvania. If not for the heroism of the passengers on flight 93, it is believed the plane would have crashed into the U.S. Capitol or the White House in Washington, D.C.

While Matthew 25 was growing, there was more violence in the news. The Branch Davidian compound came under a fifty-one-day siege by various U.S law enforcement agencies. Exchanges in gunfire killed David Koresh, the charismatic leader of the religious sect, four Federal agents, and six Davidians. During the raid, a fire broke out, killing seventy-nine additional Davidians.

The city of Los Angeles erupted in riots following the trial of Rodney King. Hurricane Mitch, the most powerful hurricane to make landfall in three hundred years, slammed into Honduras and Nicaragua—thousands died, hundreds of thousands were homeless. In Kobe, Japan, an earthquake called the Great Hanshin killed more than 6,400 people—damage estimates were ten billion dollars. In the mid-1990s, the Midwest suffered a prolonged heat wave. On five consecutive days, the mercury reached 104 degrees—3,000 people died, 750 in Chicago alone. Ted Kaczinski, the Unabomber, was captured. The channel connecting England and France was completed. Diana, the Princess of Wales, was killed in an automobile accident. Her funeral on September 6, 1997 was watched by an estimated one billion people. The next day, Mother Teresa died. The billion-dollar Hubble telescope was put into orbit, only to discover that it needed corrective lenses. Three years later, astronauts outfitted it with new prescription glasses—we could now see a universe more wondrous than most dared to imagine.

On the entertainment and political front, Sesame Street turned thirty. Delighting children and puzzling their parents, Barney, the big purple dinosaur, was an instant hit. Among the movies voted number one at the box office were *Schindler's List*, *Forrest Gump*, *Titanic*, and *Gladiator*. The wide screen lost Burt Lancaster, Audrey Hepburn, George Burns, Ginger Rogers, and Frank Sinatra. The Peanuts gang said a tearful good-bye to their creator, Charles Schultz. We lost three kings and one queen: King Hussein of Jordan (a true peacekeeper), Milton Berle (king of early television), Roy Rogers (king of the cowboys), and the Queen Mother of England. The United Kingdom handed over the sovereignty of Hong Kong to the People's Republic of China. People everywhere strained their necks to see the Hale Bopp Comet. We had two presidents, Bill Clinton and George W. Bush, each for two terms. Former President Richard Nixon died. Our planet, especially its oceans, truly lost a friend and advocate in the passing of Jacques Cousteau.

And how could we look back at the current events of our first decade without commenting on Y2K, which stands for Year 2000? Before 2000 dawned, the prophets of doom were out in full force. From 1998 to midnight 1999, not a day went by without the subject being discussed ad nauseum. We were told that our computers were ticking timebombs, ready to fail the second we entered the new year of 2000. Why? The people who brought us the computer didn't take into consideration that the computer would not be able to read 2000. The second the clock struck 2000, computers would read 1900 instead of 2000. This, we were told, would cause every computer to fail worldwide and would be more disastrous than the plagues of Egypt. There would be fighting in the streets, mass starvation, and worldwide chaos. People were frightened. Several of the young men who had families and were working for the warehouse we were leasing asked me if the doomsday predictions came true, could they have some of the rice and beans we were preparing to ship to Nicaragua? I assured them they could, and it wouldn't. Billions of dollars were spent on reprogramming computers. If you had anything to do with your company's computers, you were not at a 2000 New Year's party. You were sitting at your computer surrounded by all the other company "techs." Whatever the reason, reprogramming or pure over-hype, Y2K was certainly the biggest yawn of our first ten years. It was a fitting beginning, not only for a new decade for Matthew 25: Ministries, but a new millenium for a world capable of creating things so beautiful and doing things so ugly.

Chapter Two

Some Good News &
Some Very Bad News

Against this backdrop of world events, how did the poor, especially the children, do in our first ten years? How did we do, as Matthew 25: Ministries, in our efforts to eradicate, or at least lift some folks out of poverty?

In a few areas, there were encouraging and dramatic results. During the years of 1992-2002, fewer children under the age of five died. This was largely due to immunization efforts carried out on a massive scale. We were also elated by the news that twenty-eight million fewer children under the age of five suffered from malnutrition. Unfortunately, that was it for the positive news.

While these were hopeful statistics, the war on poverty was light-years from being won. During our first ten years, Matthew 25: Ministries won a few battles and some skirmishes against the insidious enemy of poverty and its demonic minions. However, in a report issued by the United Nations Children's Fund (UNICEF) entitled "State of the

World's Children," we were told that "children were under threat worldwide." The report confirmed what I had personally seen and heard and substantiated some grim statistics.

One billion children (one in six children) are deprived from one or more of the following: nutrition, water, sanitation, health, shelter, education, and information.

More than 16 percent of children under the age of five living in poor countries are severely malnourished, and malnutrition affects 150 million of all ages. More than 376,000 (one in five) have no close access to clean drinking water. Five hundred million children (one in three) have no sanitation facilities. Approximately 270 million children have no access to health care services. More than 265 million children have never been immunized against any childhood disease or received medical treatment. One and a half million children were orphaned by AIDS, and this number is expected to double by 2010.

More than 640 million children experience severe shelter deprivation. Almost 34 percent of children in poor countries live in dirt floor dwellings with five or more persons per room. More than 300 million school-age children, mostly girls, have never been to school. More than 300 million children are deprived of information and do not have access to television, radio, telephone, or newspapers. They only know the world beyond their villages as told to them by the adults around them, adults who often exploit their lack of knowledge and use these vulnerable children to do their diabolic bidding. Such villages are breeding grounds for terrorism.

The bottom line is that one billion people—one in six of the earth's population—live in abject poverty. One in twelve children will die before they reach their fifth birthday. The average pay or income in poor countries is less than one dollar a day. They cannot purchase the bare necessities, let alone items such as school supplies or items as inexpensive in developed countries as a bar of soap.

When Jesus said, "You will always have the poor among you . . ." (John 12:8), He did not say this to discourage us from helping the poor. He said it to remind us that poverty is a formidable foe. Jesus' life and words remind us that while we may not win the war on poverty, we must seek to win whatever battle we can. His words also carry a warning: such a fight is not for the fainthearted, the easily discouraged, the self-promoting, or for those wishing to advance a political agenda. The battle is for the humble and tireless, and for those who don't care who gets the credit. The battle belongs to foot soldiers who can take orders from the Lord and who are in it for the duration of the fight.

Yet, on such a massive global scale of human need and suffering, what impact did Matthew 25: Ministries make against such a foe in our first ten years? The only way to answer that is, again, by the numbers. Such large numbers can be hard to get our minds around, but they are an important way of measuring growth and effectiveness. Always remember that behind each number is a person who has been helped by the humanitarian aid we ship.

In our first ten years, we shipped 16,379,925 pounds of humanitarian aid in 850 forty-foot seagoing containers and aboard twenty-seven United States Air Force Reserve cargo planes. We reached our one-millionth shipped pound of aid in September 1995. Our second and third million pounds happened in April 1997 and July 1998 respectively. Our fifth millionth pound went out in 1999. By 2002 we were shipping over six million pounds each year.

We had also extended our reach beyond Nicaragua. We shipped aid to Bosnia, Kosovo, Kazakhstan, Croatia, and Afghanistan, while still shipping huge amounts of aid to Central America and the Caribbean nations. We shipped aid to an orphanage in North Korea and to hospitals in Cuba. We began a partnership with the American Indians in South Dakota and Arizona and with people in West Virginia. We also began supplying over a dozen helping agencies in Greater Cincinnati. From the Balkans to the mountains of Appalachia, from South Dakota to Cincinnati, wherever we were led and the need was great, we were there.

On that cold and dreary 2003 January day, while thanking God for sustaining us, I must confess I began to question our effectiveness. Brooding over those disturbing global statistics, I wondered deep inside what difference we were really making in such a world of need. It was not the long hours or the hard work, nor was it the finances or the never-ending search for humanitarian supplies that bothered me. No, it was always that nagging question. Were we making a difference in the lives of the "least of these?" It was then that I remembered a story, one that has many versions, but always the same core message.

One day, a slender young man was running on the beach, his cell phone in one hand, his palm pilot in his other. Like his early morning run, every moment of his life was tightly scheduled and carefully choreographed. Every second was accounted for, every second crammed full of business. Ending his phone conversation, he noticed someone ahead of him. The person's actions aroused his curiosity. It was a man who repeatedly bent over, picked something up, and threw it into the sea beyond the rushing waves. The young man stopped and asked the older man what he was doing. "Starfish," said the man. "I'm throwing back the ones stranded on the beach before the hot sun can dry them out." The sea was so vast, and the beached starfish so numerous that the young man was incredulous. Shaking his head, he said, "What difference can it make?" The older man smiled. He picked up a starfish, and as he tossed it back into the ebbing water, he said, "It made a difference to that one!"

We *were* making a difference—one person at a time. Yet, sometimes the good we were accomplishing was difficult to see and impossible to measure. Usually at our lowest moments, the voices of the skeptics would be the loudest: "What possibly can you do against such an ocean of poverty?" Then I'd visit Nicaragua and see families who once lived in cardboard shacks but now lived in modest, concrete homes built by Matthew 25: Ministries. I'd remember seeing patients who were lying on hospital beds with no mattresses or sheets; now I'd see a hospital completely furnished with mattresses and sheets, all supplied by one of our shipments. I'd remember doctors who operated in their street clothes on patients in theirs; now I'd see doctors and patients wearing surgical and patient gowns furnished by another Matthew 25: Ministries' shipment. I'd remember clinics that once had empty shelves and women who were examined on rough, splintered boards propped up by concrete blocks; now I'd see clinics with the shelves full of medical supplies and equipped with new examination tables. I'd remember hungry and naked children who were now being fed and clothed, children going to school with needed school supplies. I'd visit the dairy cooperative we started with ten cows, which grew into a herd of one hundred sixty cows that enabled the entire village to pay off its debt, provide income to the families, and milk for their children. I'd see the schools we rebuilt and the community centers we built.

Then I'd say with confidence, "Yes, Lord, we are making a difference."

Little did I know then that 2003 would usher in a time of unprecedented growth for Matthew 25: Ministries. In faith, we went looking for another, larger warehouse. What size did we need? I didn't know, but I just didn't believe our accelerated growth was a fluke. All the signs pointed to a period of even greater growth. We found a larger warehouse and signed a one-year lease. This was our eighth warehouse in ten years. Our new landlord gently tried to coax me into signing a three-year lease for a considerable discount. In the past I would have jumped at the offer, but not this time. Something inside of me said, "Don't sign," so I didn't.

Our new warehouse (which we called Highland after the street it was on) was the largest we had ever occupied, or needed. We now were working out of a clean, 80,000-square-foot warehouse. The location was fair, and truck accessibility was good. The neighborhood was safe for staff and volunteers. The Highland warehouse did come with some sticker shock, however. It would be our most expensive lease ever. The new Highland lease was $17,000 a month. The mortgage payment on the Loveland facility was $5,000 each month. Together, we were paying more than $260,000 each year in lease and mortgage payments. The year before, we just barely made the $12,000 monthly lease payment at the Swallen's warehouse. I took a deep breath and said, "Lord, I hope you know what I am doing!"

After signing the lease, I stood alone in the Highland warehouse, staring at the keys in my hand. With each new warehouse, I always asked the same questions: "How are we ever going to fill this place? How are we ever going to pay for this place? When are we ever going to have a home of our own?" You can never pay off a lease. If we had a place we owned and we were debt free, just think of all the good we could do for the poor with that extra money! I turned off the lights and left our pricey new warehouse.

Chapter Three

Warehousing: The Leviticus Promise

In the Hebrew Old Testament, it is called *asamim*. In the Greek New Testament, the closest word is t*ameion*. In Spanish, they say *bodega* and in English, we call it a warehouse. Simply defined, a warehouse is "a building in which goods and merchandise are stored." The concept of the warehouse dates back to the early days of the Old Testament.

In Genesis, we read that famine had spread throughout the land and Joseph opened up the storehouses, or warehouses (41:56).

The story of Joseph is as familiar as it is old. The favorite son of his father, Jacob, Joseph was sold into slavery by his jealous brothers. The father was told that a ferocious beast killed Joseph. Their evidence? Joseph's ornate coat which they smeared with the blood of a goat. Jacob wept bitterly. No one, not even Joseph, could have known that God would save a people and create a nation with this lone despicable act. As my friend the Reverend

Mike Brandy used to say, "God often points straight with a crooked stick."

Joseph eventually landed in an Egyptian prison, accused of a crime he did not commit. Through his steadfast faith in God and his ability to interpret dreams, he became "the favorite" again, this time of none other than the Pharaoh. "Then the Pharaoh said to Joseph, 'I am Pharaoh, but without your word no one will lift hand or foot in all of Egypt'" (Gen. 41:44). Pharaoh then gave Joseph the critical job of developing an agriculture program for the next fourteen years. The first seven years would be a time of plenty, the next seven would be years of famine. Pharaoh dreamed it, Joseph interpreted it, and now Joseph would execute the plan.

Joseph wasted no time. During the seven years of plenty, he bought up all the surplus grain, no doubt at rock bottom prices. He built large storehouses in key cities and stored in them the food grown in surrounding fields. The Bible tells us that the harvest was so vast they "stopped keeping records because it was beyond measure" (Gen. 41:49). When the seven years of famine fell on the land, Joseph was prepared to face the crisis and profit by it.

After the first of seven failed harvests, people ran out of food and began showing up in Egypt from surrounding countries for "the famine was severe in all the world" (Gen. 41:57). Long lines of hungry and desperate people formed in front of Pharaoh's palace.

Pharaoh told the people to go see Joseph, which they did. Interestingly, Joseph didn't give the grain away. The people purchased the grain with money, then livestock, and finally land. They begged for seed, which Joseph sold them, provided they gave to Pharaoh one-fifth of the crops each year. The famine also reunited Joseph with his family. Driven by hunger they, too, came to Egypt. Joseph forgave his brothers and gave his family property in a high rent district of Egypt. Everything they needed, they received.

Four centuries after Joseph, Moses said to the Israelites, "The Lord will send a blessing on your barns [storehouses] and on everything you put your hand to" (Deut. 28:8). It was a sign of God's favor when storehouses were full, especially overflowing. Later, during the reigns of the three righteous kings, (David, Jehoshaphat, and Hezekiah) storehouses were built throughout the land in strategically designated "store cities." These storehouses were needed to accommodate the abundant harvest that was seen as a blessing from God. These overflowing storehouses were also seen as a sign from God that these three kings were in God's favor because of their obedience and faith in Him.

Throughout the United States, corporations maintain strategically located warehouses which occupy more than one-and-a-half-billion square feet. Warehouse workers remain busy filling and emptying an estimated thirty-nine million trucks. Warehousing is crucial to our economy and commerce. Without warehouses, we would have no way of getting goods to the stores and, ultimately, to our homes and places of work. Little has changed over the past three millennia. The basic concept of modern day warehouses is the same as the storehouses we read about in the Bible. Then, as well as now, goods are received, processed, inventoried, stored, and then shipped to points of sale: grocery and hardware stores, home and garden centers. There is one basic difference between warehouses of yesterday and those of today. In biblical times, an overflowing storehouse was seen as a blessing; not today. Today, corporations want goods coming and going in a timely, scheduled manner. The system breaks down when they cannot move items for a variety of reasons, i.e., scuffed labels or mislabeled, over-runs, damaged packaging, buyouts. Such goods take up an incredible amount of space. Companies are faced with the need to quickly liquidate these products at greatly reduced costs, or if necessary, send the items to the landfill. Here is where Matthew 25: Ministries steps in. Companies can donate their "distressed" products to Matthew 25: Ministries. The corporation receives a tax write-off, saves the landfill, guarantees their products are shipped out of the United States (if necessary), and most important, helps the poor. You could not ask for a bigger win/win situation.

One day while I was being interviewed for a television program, I was asked to sum up what we do. I said, "We are garbage pickers for the Lord." We certainly do not send garbage to the poor—80 percent of everything we ship is brand new. Rather, we save products from becoming garbage by positioning ourselves between corporations with distressed products and the landfill.

When people visit our warehouse and hear how we rescue ten million pounds of products from the landfill each year, they say, "Oh, how wasteful we Americans are." I always respond by saying that we are only wasteful if it gets to the landfill. No matter how carefully you prepare a meal, leftovers are inevitable. God is merely asking us to share those leftovers with the poor. Later we will see how God wants us to give out of our poverty, but here He is asking that we give out of our abundance. It's true: we can care for a needy world with the things we would throw away.

Here's how it works:

One day, a call came into our office. It was from a well-known shoe company that was shutting down its huge distribution facility in Cincinnati. For many reasons, mostly logistical and timing, they did not want to sell the shoes to a discount buyer, but wanted to give them to a charity. "What size is the donation?" I asked. "Two to three hundred thousand pairs," the man replied. Tears of worry and joy filled my eyes. Worry, because this would be our biggest donation ever. Would we be able to handle it? Joy, because of all the shoeless people I had seen during my trips. People who had no shoes and certainly never had a new pair of shoes would now have shoes. "Can you handle such an order?" he persisted. After a brief prayer, I said an unqualified, "Yes!" "Can we start shipping immediately and complete the transfer within the month?" he wanted to know. "Sure," I answered, thinking to myself, *How are we ever going to do this?*

The shoes began to arrive at the fifth warehouse we were occupying. We called it the Old Ford Plant, or Red Bank Road warehouse. The shoes were all new, still in their boxes. They were complete with tissue paper and paper stuffed into their toes. We were afraid the shoes would all be size 13EEE. To our surprise, they were shoes we could ship to refugee camps, rural villages, the American Indians in South Dakota, and the needy of Cincinnati—we could ship everywhere.

We received the shoes during the hottest part of the summer. The shoes came ten to eighteen pairs per box. All the boxes were floor-loaded, which meant we could not use a forklift because they were not on pallets. We had to carry them off the trucks by hand and place them on pallets on the dock floor. There they were plastic wrapped, labeled, and then forklifted to their space in the warehouse. We were also putting them into categories so we would not ship the same type and size shoes to the same places.

The one month stretched into three months due to glitches by the company, not us. The company also kept finding more shoes they wanted to donate. After it was all said and done, we unloaded more than seventy semis—a donation of nine hundred thousand pairs of shoes. We were exhausted but exhilarated. Our warehouse system worked. We stayed with our basic operating principles and proved that we could handle huge donations.

Within a few months, we moved into a larger warehouse in the same area, the Swallen's warehouse. Each time we moved, I would go alone and dedicate the warehouse to God and then, if physically possible, I'd walk the inside perimeter seven times as the Israelites did around Jericho (Josh. 6:15), not to make walls come tumbling down, but to fill the warehouse up wall-to-wall.

As we became larger and things accelerated to an unbelievably hectic pace, often I felt like the father in the Gospels who brought his son to Jesus. The boy would throw himself down, convulsing and foaming at the mouth. The father pleaded with Jesus to do something. Jesus said, "Everything is possible for him who believes." To which this troubled father said, "I do believe, help me overcome my unbelief" (Mark 9:23–24).

When people hear the story of Matthew 25: Ministries, they often tell me that I must have great faith. Like that father, I have times when my faith is ambivalent. It is at such times that I am sustained by God's promise. It is what I call the "Leviticus Promise."

> I will look on you with favor and make you fruitful and increase your numbers, and I will keep my covenant with you. You will still be eating last year's harvest when you will have to move it out to make room for the new [harvest].
>
> Lev. 26:9–10

To paraphrase, if you work hard and place your trust in God, you don't have to worry about next year's harvest, wondering if it will be plentiful. In faith, use up what is in your storehouses and trust that He will fill them to over-flowing again.

Chapter Four

The Nomadic Life

He did not possess the wisdom of Solomon nor the courage of David. He did not have the strength of Samson, the leadership of Gideon, or the bravery of Elijah. He did not demonstrate the prophetic powers of Isaiah or Jeremiah. He was not always honorable, did not have the power to interpret dreams as did Joseph, and was not virtuous as was Daniel. There is no evidence that he built or wrote anything. And yet he is revered by Christians, Muslims, and Jews. He stands alone when it comes to faith. No one in all of the Old Testament possessed a greater faith in God than this man.

In his seventy-fifth year, God came to him and made this promise. "If you have faith in me, I will bless you and make you into a great nation" (Gen. 12:1–3, paraphrase). So he took his wife, Sarah, nephew Lot, extended family, and all his possessions and set out on a journey of faith unparalleled in all the Old Testament. Until his last

breath, he lived the life of a nomad, a wanderer, whose
entire life was guided by faith alone. He would never again
call any place home. His name was Abram, but God
changed it to Abraham.

Before all the warehouses we leased, before there was
even a thought of starting up a humanitarian effort, before
we even contemplated naming it Matthew 25: Ministries, I
went with a team of doctors and nurses to Nicaragua in
January 1990. A part of me wanted to go because of the
adventure, a larger part of me felt that God was calling me
to step out in faith and visit this war-torn country. I didn't
realize it then, but that trip would be the beginning of a
fourteen-year nomadic life. Until then, I was a person who
made sure I knew where I would land before I jumped. The
very idea of living like Abraham was not appealing to me;
such a life came with too many uncertainties.

The call to Nicaragua occurred when the war between
the Contras and Sandinistas was still raging, primarily in
the mountains along the Honduran border. Nicaragua was
certainly not a tourist attraction. It was a dangerous place
under any circumstances. My wife, Mickey, and children
Tim, Clare, and Aaron, had a great many reservations about
me going. They were constantly on my mind during the
trip. But because of the way the trip unfolded, I firmly
believed God wanted me to go, and I went on faith.

Aside from being detained when we stepped off the
plane in the capital city of Managua for visa irregularities,
the trip went as planned. While I had grown-up in the

inner city, worked as a social worker, and later as an inner-city pastor, I thought I had seen poverty. Nothing I had seen prepared me for the poverty I saw in that city of one million people.

I visited a cholera ward and saw two men sharing the last IV bag. I prayed with men in an infectious disease ward, knowing full well that if their immune system did not kill their disease, they would surely die. The hospital had no drugs, not even penicillin. After touring a 450-bed hospital, we were taken to the director's office. She told us not to touch anything with our hands, especially our faces. After we waited more than ten minutes, a nurse came in with a bar of soap in one hand and keys in another. We were then instructed to wash our hands before we left the hospital. Later, I learned that soap was so scarce that it was literally kept under lock and key.

Inflation was so high that a suitcase of the Nicaraguan currency, the córdoba, was needed to buy a loaf of bread. Unemployment ran as high as 60 percent. The poorest were living on a cup of rice a day. Managua's utilities were unreliable, which was disastrous for hospitals. Water would go off without warning. We never went anywhere at night without flashlights. The hospitals were always full. Thousands of land mines were still buried and unaccounted for after the war. Those who stepped on them were maimed and horribly disfigured for life. The victims were mostly children. Most of the schools were shut down because the students had no supplies. School buildings were either totally collapsed or were in the process of collapsing. The scars of the 1972 earthquake, which completely destroyed downtown Managua, were still very visible. Partially collapsed high rises became housing for people who had no other place to live. The police had given up chasing the people away from these dangerous buildings. The people just kept coming back. The slightest tremor threatened to bring down these buildings at any moment. The need for some type of roof over their heads outweighed the fear of losing their lives. It was a gamble and they were willing to take it. They had no money and no other option.

One day, I was riding around Managua in the back of a pickup truck. As a pastor, I always tried to follow the advice that when there was great sorrow and sadness, I could "sip but never swallow." I should not be distant or uncaring, but as a pastor I must keep my composure so that I could minister effectively to those going through distress and sorrow. That day, I took more than a sip.

As we drove through the city, I thought of the Old Testament prophet Ezekiel. He really was not supposed to be a prophet. He was actually called to be a priest, as was his father and all their fathers before them. Ezekiel and his father faithfully served God and His people in the great temple built by Solomon in the holy city of Jerusalem. Ezekiel lived during the final tumultuous days of the southern kingdom of Judah. The northern kingdom, Israel, lay in ruin. Now Judah's worst nightmare was about to come true. When Ezekiel celebrated his thirtieth birthday, the age when a man could become a priest, the full might of the dreaded Babylonian army fell upon Judah. King Nebuchadnezzar gave orders to slaughter large numbers of those in Judah and to destroy the temple. He also deported thousands of the Israelites to Babylon. During their forced march, thousands died of starvation and disease. Ezekiel and his family were a part of this historical exile.

Serving as both prophet and priest to the exiles, one day Ezekiel came upon a pitiful and deeply disturbing sight. A group of diseased, starving, and homeless exiles had taken up residence on the muddy banks of the Kebar River. Such poverty he had never seen, such despair he had never witnessed. In his journal he made this notation " . . . and there, where they were living, I sat among them for seven days—overwhelmed" (Ezek. 3:15).

I felt like Ezekiel. God was calling me to these people. I was totally, completely overwhelmed. I felt like I was suffocating. I resisted, then I yielded to God. I knew that this was a defining moment in my life and that I was being called by God to help the Nicaraguans who were living in such poverty.

What I did not know was that I was in for a long nomadic journey. As with Abraham, it would be a journey of faith strengthening and faith testing. While the journey at times would seem to be aimless, I believed it was divinely guided. I needed to learn many things. Mainly, I needed to learn to trust and rely completely upon God and follow the path He had laid before me. God was going to take me to places I did not want to go so that He could get me to places He wanted me to be.

During our first ten years, we wandered in and out of nine warehouses. Our finances went up and down. Plans were made, plans were changed. Disagreements arose, people left, new people came aboard. I often grasped for a sense of permanence, which was always beyond my reach. Facing such constant changes, I'd often think how the life of the nomad was not a life for me. The feeling of being over-whelmed never quite left me, although I was becoming more confident that we were going in the right direction.

At the end of the day, what kept me going was that taste in my mouth I experienced in the back of that pickup in Managua. I went against the advice given me. I didn't take a little sip; I took a gargantuan swallow. It burned my mouth and hurt going down. That day I developed a case of "poverty reflux." All that I was experiencing and the sacrifices I was making paled in comparison, however, to what the people in poverty stricken countries such as Nicaragua were experiencing each day. My problem in keeping Matthew 25: Ministries going and providing for my family were merely inconveniences compared to their daily struggles to just survive. If God had called me to be a nomad, then so be it.

Chapter Five

The Southern Route

O ne of the greatest stories in literature, certainly in the entire Bible, is the story of Moses' confrontation with Pharaoh and Moses' famous words, "Let my people go!" After a series of plagues, Pharaoh finally relented and granted the Israelites their freedom. This ended their four-hundred-year stay in Egypt. Since coming to Egypt, during the days of Joseph, they have grown into the nation promised to Abraham.

During the great Exodus of the Israelites, Pharaoh had a change of heart and desired revenge for the death of his son who was killed by the tenth and last plague. His officials also pointed out that if the Israelites were permitted to leave, they would lose a large, cheap labor force. Pharaoh led his entire army against Moses and the Israelites. With Pharaoh's army behind and the Red Sea ahead, the people panicked and blamed Moses for the looming disaster.

The Israelites' lack of faith was a constant irritant to Moses, and the reason why he had so many long, arduous talks with God. And always, he heard the same words when things didn't go their way, "It would have been better for us to serve the Egyptians than to die in the desert" (Exod. 14:12).

Moses raised his staff, stretched out his hand, the Red Sea parted, and the people hurried to the other side. Once all had made it safely across, Pharaoh's army was completely destroyed by the receding water. Everyone was wild with excitement. "All's right with the world, now on to the Promised Land!" Here the story took an interesting and often overlooked turn.

Moses could have taken two routes to the Promised Land. The northern route was the one taken by caravans going back and forth from Egypt and Canaan and was known as the land "flowing with milk and honey." The trip would have only taken a few months. . . . "Hmm, let's see, there was the Exodus, the parting of the Red Sea, and now a leisurely three-to-six-week journey to the Promised Land. Life does not get any better," the Israelites surely must have been thinking. Instead, God instructed Moses to head south.

Why not the northern route? It was the quickest way to the Promised Land. Simple. God said, "If they face war, they might change their minds and return to Egypt" (Exod. 13:17). So, Moses led the people back toward the Red Sea. What do you think their response was? Based upon their actions so far, I'm certain it wasn't, "Three cheers for Moses!" It didn't make any sense to them. Their destination was the Promised Land. Why not take the quickest route possible? Not the southern route, that led away from where they were told God wanted them to be. I'm sure they tried to talk Moses out of what seemed a ridiculous plan. They no doubt brought up the fact that they hadn't known their leader, Moses, very long. They were impressed with the parting of the Red Sea, the thing with the plagues, and standing up to Pharaoh the way he did. But there was this invisible God, who only Moses could speak to and who gave Moses his marching orders. They had just met this God. Moses had to tell them His name, and anyway, what kind of a name is "I AM WHO I AM" or "Yahweh" for a god? The Egyptians had many gods with cool names: Osiris, Amun, and Hotep, to mention a few. These gods were not invisible or shy. Their likenesses were plastered all over palace walls, carved into every monument, and appeared in all the burial chambers. Moses' God and everything about Him had been lost for over four hundred years. Taking the southern route, on the word of a man they had just met and a God they couldn't see, was asking a lot.

Four hundred years ago they had cozied down in Egypt, taking advantage of Joseph's status. They lived in a place called Goshen, in Egypt, thinking that this would be their permanent home. At the end of those four centuries, Joseph was a faded memory and why they were there, no one really knew. They had forsaken their tribal heritage and they did not know or acknowledge the God of their ancestors. They had been foreigners in a strange land all along, with no shared history to bind them and no vision to guide them.

There is also the human factor. Humans tend to take the path that is most comfortable. The northern route was

shorter than the southern, and the topography was not as
forbidding. The necessities of life, such as food and water,
would be difficult to come by in the desert. Everything indicated that going south was a bad idea. Besides, they thought,
"There are a lot of us. We can take care of ourselves. We are
not a bunch of wimps. We won't run if there is a fight."

A compromise of sorts was reached. They would take
the southern route through the deserts of Shur, down to
the Wilderness of Sinai, pick up the Ten Commandments,
and then head north to the Promised Land.

On their three-month journey to Mt. Sinai, they
experienced a few "this-is-the-reason-God-didn't-think-
you-were-ready-for-the-northern-route" moments. Not
even three days after the parting of the Red Sea, they
began grumbling because they could not find any water,
and then when they did, it was bitter. So God sweetened
the water (Exod. 15:22–24). One-and-a-half months later,
while traveling through the Desert of Sin, they cried out
to Moses that they wanted meat to eat, and again they
whined, "If only we died by the LORD's hand in Egypt!"
(Exod. 16:3). So God gave them quail and daily provisions of manna to eat for as many days that their journey
in the wilderness would take. So that they wouldn't get
lost, He provided them with a pillar of cloud by day and
a pillar of fire by night to guide them (Exod. 13:21).

Then we have the whole fiasco at Mt. Sinai. Moses
went up the mountain to receive the Ten Commandments.
The people worried about his lengthy absence and talked
Moses' brother, Aaron, into helping them make an object
to worship. It was an image of one of the Egyptian gods,
the golden calf.

When Moses descended from Mt. Sinai carrying the Ten Commandments and saw this spectacle before him, we can confidently say he was not a happy camper. Aaron stood shrugging his shoulders and mouthing the words, "They made me do it." The people dancing around the idol had worked themselves up into a feverish pitch. Oh, how fragile was the bond of trust between Moses and the Israelites. In a fit of anger, he threw down the tablets, breaking them into pieces, and he administered harsh punishment to the guilty. He climbed the mountain again, received another set of the Commandments, and the journey continued.

Finally, the southern route took a northern turn. They passed through the Wilderness of Paran, came to the Wilderness of Zin, and made camp at the edge of the Promised Land. It had been about five years since leaving Egypt. They thought they had their act together. The twelve tribes of the Israelites were a cohesive group. They had learned to follow Moses. They built God a tabernacle, or "tent of meeting," and carried before them the Ark of the Covenant. God had been faithful. They had learned to trust Him, but was that trust strong enough for what lay ahead? Had five years been sufficient to prepare them for the biggest challenge they would face so far?

At a place called Kadesh, twelve men (one from each tribe) came back and reported to Moses and the entire assembly what they saw when they spied out the Promised Land. Indeed, it was a land flowing with milk and honey. The vote, however, was ten to two against the idea that the Israelites were strong enough to defeat the people who inhabited the Promised Land. Joshua and Caleb cast the minority vote in favor of taking the Land. The two men tried, without success, to calm down the people and convince them that they could take the Promised Land. But when the ten said that the people living there were so huge (compared to them) that they felt like grasshoppers (Num. 13:33), the Israelites were filled with fear and cried out for Moses to be replaced. Once again, they complained that the troubles they faced in Egypt were a piece of cake compared to this.

For their lack of faith, they were sentenced to stay in the wilderness one year for each of the forty days the twelve men spied out the Promised Land. That would be a total of forty years, five they had already spent getting this far, plus thirty-five more.

Why did this happen? Simple. They were not prepared. The Promised Land was ready for them, but they were not ready for it. If they had their way, they would have tried to get there five years before the Kadesh experience by taking the northern route. One can only imagine what would have happened if God would have permitted it then. They were not prepared to take the northern route when they left Egypt, and they weren't ready after spending five years in the wilderness. They would only be ready when God said they were ready, which meant forty years in the wilderness traveling the symbolic southern route.

Looking back, I see how so unprepared we were in the early days of Matthew 25: Ministries. We questioned why the supplies were slow coming in, the financial resources meager, and what seemed like a never-ending trek from one warehouse to another. The need was so great and the situation urgent. People's lives were at stake. Why was everything so hard and the path so strewn with obstacles? Well, that huge donation of new shoes and many such donations to follow were ready for us, but we were not ready for them. If God allowed us to take the quick and easy "northern route," we would have failed and probably damaged our credibility with corporations. For ten years, God took us in and out of warehouses. We developed our skills and our basic system for receiving, handling, and shipping supplies. We have tested the system with small, large, and gigantic donations, and we still use it today.

At the beginning of 2003, I believed we were close to the Promised Land. We had been tried and tested. I also believed that our nomadic days were coming to an end. A gathering of people and events had taken place that assured me that our wilderness trek was about over and we were concluding our "southern route."

Chapter Six

The Search Is On

While 2002, statistically, was a record-breaking year, it was also a year in which circumstances led me to believe that God was up to something. What? I did not know, but (to quote Alice in Wonderland), things were getting "curiouser and curiouser."

We did attempt to purchase a warehouse during our first ten years, one we leased from February 2001 to April 2002. It was an interesting building with a fascinating history.

The building was actually part of the Swallen's Department Store complex. In 1948, Wilbur F. "Pat" Swallen opened up a discount store in his home. Pat was a warm, caring Christian businessman who brought high ethical standards to the marketplace. Five years later, he outgrew his basement and garage and built his first store. Pat had a well-deserved reputation in Greater Cincinnati for providing quality merchandise at the lowest prices. The Swallen's stores were no-frills stores with concrete floors and exposed duct work, but they were known for their knowledgeable sales personnel. During the 1960–1980s, there was not a store in Greater Cincinnati with a better name recognition than Swallen's.

Sadly, in November 1988, Pat died of a stroke. The family sold the business in April 1995. In the summer of 1996, all the Swallen's property was sold at auction.

There is an interesting footnote to the story of Pat Swallen and how he touched my life one Wednesday evening in the mid-1960s.

During the 1950s, most Protestant Christians would go to church services, listen, be quiet, and go home. The only sounds they made were singing the congregational hymns, and their only participation was taking up the offering and giving out communion. All of the rest—the preaching, visitation, and running the church—was the job of the clergy. In August 1965, Keith Miller wrote his revolutionary and best-selling book, *A Taste of New Wine.* Thus began the church renewal movement. To those who didn't live in the '60s, the radical nature of this book and the movement it launched cannot be appreciated. Likewise, most would find what Keith Miller advocates commonplace today because so many of the beliefs and ideas have been assimilated into the church.

Miller made the case that the work of the church is not the sole responsibility of the clergy, but instead belonged to the clergy and the laity alike. Also, the church had become stale and lifeless. It was old wine in old wineskins. The wine was sour (the church's message) and the wineskins (the church) were ready to burst open. My own modern-day spin on this idea is that the clergy needs to be about the business of equipping and sending out the saints for ministry and the church, the people of God, need to be engaged in ministry 24/7.

All over the United States, groups of people were coming together to study and talk about *A Taste of New Wine*. It was an exciting time, and during one of these group meetings I received a call from God on my life and eventually became a pastor.

Many clergy were threatened by the church renewal movement. My pastor was not; quite the contrary, he embraced it. Along with the group meeting, my pastor started a Wednesday potluck dinner and brought in speakers. One of those speakers was Pat Swallen. I know for many, the idea of a layman talking about his faith doesn't seem like a big deal; it's done all the time today. More laymen speak and write about their faith today than do clergy. But in the 1960s, this was a momentous occasion. He spoke with such conviction and passion and encouraged us to take our faith with us wherever we went. He then told a story I've never forgotten.

Pat didn't use any names and assured us that only he and his accountant knew about this story. He said that his accountant told him that someone was stealing money from the company. After a lengthy investigation, to their great disbelief, they discovered the thief: a woman who had worked at the store since it opened. Her financial pressures at home had become too much, and Pat said she gave into temptation and began taking home more than her salary. He understood, but did not justify what she did. "If only she would've come to me," he lamented. He did not have her arrested. Instead, he transferred her to another department and deducted from her check until the amount she had stolen was repaid.

I'm not saying that his payback method should be followed; I just wanted to show that Pat Swallen was a Christian who took his faith into his work-a-day world. His story encouraged us to do the same.

The warehouse we leased was where the Swallen Store housed all its electrical appliances and large items like stereos, mattresses, and refrigerators. This was the building where people went to pick up their purchases. Since most items would fit in a car or truck, there were only a couple of docks. The building was not heated. Picking up purchases was a cold transaction in the winter. When Swallen's closed, the warehouse was purchased separately from the other buildings in the complex. The new owners put in a heating system and twelve docks. When we moved in we were in dock heaven.

The walls were constructed out of preformed concrete panels, quite an innovation for the time. The walls were not insulated, which made heating an expensive proposition. The company that purchased the warehouse installed a heating system, which much to our dismay was terribly expensive to operate. After we had the system serviced in the fall, the technician said, "You are going to be in for a sticker shock," and were we ever!

The other fascinating feature about our eighth warehouse was that a stream ran underneath the building. The warehouse had been built over a creek. How this was ever approved by the city, no one will never know. For most of the year it was a dry creek bed, but in the spring it could become a raging torrent. It once came to within six inches of the building's floor. I asked someone who used to work there if the water ever came into the building. He replied simply, "Close!"

Except for the heating system, the building was ideal. It had everything we needed—size, location, docks, and a large parking lot. I asked Michael Brandy, a friend of mine who was in the real-estate business, if he could give me some advice on how to make an offer to purchase the building. We quickly discovered that the owner valued the building a great deal more than we or the market did. Our first bid was four hundred thousand dollars less than what he thought was a reasonable price.

Back and forth we went—offers and counter offers for six months. Then something happened which I'm certain Alice would find most "curiouser." Our lease was up and we asked if we could stay on a monthly basis until we found somewhere else to go. I did not want to move into another warehouse temporarily. I told him we'd pay what we were paying and would only ask for a thirty-day notice. He turned us down. One realtor said he surely must have someone standing in the wings to turn down such an offer, which was not the case. The building sat vacant for over one year. Why did this happen? In hindsight, I believe that it was a God thing. I truly thought we had a home of our own; all signs pointed to this place. But it was as if God pulled a veil down over this man's eyes, who I knew to be a good man and a Christian.

I was extremely disappointed that we did not get the Swallen's warehouse. It was certainly my heart's desire. I was determined more than ever to find us a home of our own. It was not a matter of pride of accomplishment or ending the constant moving from one warehouse to another. My concern was always the enormous amount we were paying to lease, money which could go to the poor. The attempt to purchase the Swallen's building motivated us to continue looking.

Chapter Seven

The Gathering of Men

Two significant events took place that brought two men to Matthew 25: Ministries. Their skills and dedication would play a crucial role in our search for and acquisition of a warehouse.

First, my dear friend and colleague, the Rev. Mike Brandy, died of heart problems which he had bravely fought for several years. Mike's death was a huge loss to his family, friends, to Matthew 25: Ministries, and to me personally. Regardless of the situation or person, Mike always found a way to talk about the work of Matthew 25: Ministries. He was one of our best ambassadors, and he is deeply missed. But I have found that God never takes someone without sending someone to take his or her place. After his death, Mike's son, Michael, became more and more active in Matthew 25: Ministries.

After college, Michael started his own company, Brandicorp, which specialized in commercial real-estate development, restaurant, and hospitality. Brandicorp worked with national franchises and won numerous awards. It continued real-estate development for such national businesses as Kroger's, Walgreen's, Shell, and Starbucks. Michael was highly respected by his peers and employees, and Brandicorp was a profitable company with low management turnover.

Michael was a pro when it came to real estate and finances. He also had a heart for the poor and felt a need to give back, which he did through his church, community, and now Matthew 25: Ministries. He picked up the mantle his father laid down. I asked Michael if he would serve as chairman of our board of directors and help me pursue a warehouse. He said yes! With our precarious finances, we knew finding a warehouse we could afford would take a miracle. We kept reminding ourselves that miracles were God's specialty. We needed to find and purchase a warehouse, and God sent us a man who specialized in real estate and finance.

Michael told me on several occasions about his friend, Dave Knust. Michael believed he would be a wonderful asset to our work. Dave was also a pro when it came to just about anything electrical and mechanical. Just like Michael, Dave was living the American dream. Know-how and a lot of hard work are the ingredients of success. As the saying goes, the only place success comes before work is in the dictionary, and it was certainly true with these two men.

I had the opportunity to meet Dave, all 6 foot 4 inches of him. A graduate of Moeller High School, Dave had received a Bachelor of Science degree in Industrial

Management. He worked for a variety of companies: General Motors, the Ford Corporation, Avon. He discovered that his childhood hobby of taking things apart and putting them back together to see how they worked paid off later in life. He enjoyed every aspect of manufacturing and was a plant engineer wherever he worked. He had sold his business and was looking for something meaningful to do with his time. I was as taken with his pleasant personality as I was with Michael's humility.

I believe that everything we do in life will be used by God somehow, someway, in the future. That has always proven true for me. For example, I was unable to decide what I wanted my major to be in college, so I signed up for an introductory course in economics. The professor's enthusiasm got my attention, and soon I was majoring in economics, concentrating in global and industrial economics. I remember taking all those college field trips to manufacturing and distribution centers, thinking that they were interesting, but wondering when I'd ever use industrial or global economics. When I graduated, I became a social worker with the welfare department, then went to seminary. After graduation, I became pastor of a small inner-city church. Soon, I was on many boards and committees that dealt with multi-million-dollar budgets. I couldn't have realized how all this would be used.

So now, Matthew 25: Ministries had a man who knew finance and real estate and another who knew warehouses and could fix anything that had a motor attached. God was gathering these men and women to do something wonderful. All of our skills and life experiences were going to be called upon.

Later in 2003, I had lunch with Michael and Dave. I asked Dave to join us in looking for a warehouse to purchase. I told them that I believed God had brought us together for this specific reason. I also told them that I believed God was on the move, and I didn't want to be left behind. The area where the warehouse would be located needed to be convenient and safe for our volunteers and accessible for our truck traffic. I felt we needed to stay south of I-275, and somewhere in the northeast area, which stretched from Tri County on the west to Milford on the east. Traveling like a nomad for the last eleven years, I had the opportunity to see many warehouses and locations and developed a sense of what would and would not work. I also felt that God had given me these instructions, just like he gave the Israelites the precise measurements for building the tabernacle in the wilderness. After giving these specifications I'd often hear, "I don't know if we'll ever find what you are looking for where you're looking!" Dave said he'd be happy to help.

Some of the more notable warehouses and properties we looked at: The Hauck Road warehouse was 120,000 square feet, move-in ready, twelve docks, and perfect, but too pricey at $3.5 million. We walked some land just off I-275 with great visibility, but not big enough to meet our eighty-thousand-square-feet requirement. We looked east at property in Milford. The price was reasonable, and main access was the interstate off-ramp, which was great for trucks, but bad for volunteers. We looked at property in Norwood which needed to be razed, not sold. We toured a gigantic warehouse that had forty-foot ceilings and a roof held up by the inside racking. We'd need a

$250,000 specialized piece of equipment to retrieve pallets on the rack. Another warehouse was too large and too chopped up. I even looked at a place in Newtown, Ohio, which was too far and inconvenient—you'd have to pass out maps to find the place. We looked at every vacant warehouse, especially in the Blue Ash area, which fell in the parameters I had given. Nothing.

It was frustrating. There were some warehouses I thought were a slam dunk to become ours, but for whatever reason the deal would go south. I was ready to sign a long-term lease at the Highland warehouse when something happened, something truly amazing. And definitely a message from God.

We had no real estate agent under contract. We had no "for sale" sign in front of the Loveland building, a 15,000-square-feet facility which we built six years before and was now serving as our headquarters. Within a month three groups—two churches and a business—walked in the front door and asked if our building was for sale. They all said the same thing: They had heard we were thinking of selling, were driving by, and thought they'd stop in.

Coincidental? Perhaps to some. Providential? Most definitely, to us. God sent those groups to us during a time of discouragement. After months and months of looking and not being willing to budge on the parameters, I began to think maybe we should look at signing a longer, cheaper lease and resign ourselves to the fact that it was a nomadic life for us—at least for now. Then three knocks came to our front door, asking if our building was for sale. Frankly, we had spent all of our time looking for another warehouse.

We had not thought about selling the Loveland property. God was moving ahead of us, and we'd better catch up.

While we didn't have a warehouse to purchase or even one in sight, we felt we needed to sell the Loveland building and land. Talk about putting the cart before the horse! We also decided to put together a capital campaign—a campaign to buy what? Well, God hadn't shown us yet. But, if we were able to sell the Loveland building and grounds, we'd have some liquid assets. Michael started the process of securing a loan. We didn't have an inkling of how much this warehouse—which we hadn't found despite three years of looking—was going to cost when we did find it. It was the kind of thinking every banker loves to hear! Michael also worked with the three interested parties who wanted to purchase the Loveland building. The first offer came in at exactly the price we wanted, but didn't think we'd get.

Our plan was shaped like a pie cut in three pieces, all necessary for success. We needed to sell the Loveland facility, raise a certain amount of money through a capital campaign, and obtain a significant corporate grant. Michael was working on the first piece. If he succeeded and closed quickly on the deal, we'd most certainly be living in tents like the Israelites. That was okay. We had lived and worked out of worse places. We had served our symbolic forty years and were ready for God to lead us home.

Chapter Eight

Providence

The word "providence" does not appear often in the Greek New Testament, yet more than ten words are used to describe it, all with a slightly different meaning. For example, *hetoimazo* means "has provided," *ktaomai* means "to get," and *paristemi,* "to present." The word that I believe best describes providence is *pronoia*. It means "forethought." This agrees with the Latin *providentia*, which also means forethought. When we look at the modern English translation, we find that providence means "to care or make preparations in advance." A word that I believe is interchangeable with providence is "provision."

As a person of faith, I do not believe things happen randomly. Fate and all its siblings: good fortune, chances, odds, roll of the dice, blind luck, luck of the draw, or happenstance, are not how I see the world operates. I believe that God is not only there before we arrive, but has provisions laid up for us for our journey. He has answered our prayers even before we asked them. He has removed obstacles before we reach them or helps us get in shape to overcome them. He has gone ahead of us to bring together the people we need to meet before we knew we needed to meet them. Divine providence is God's will in action.

Providence can be misunderstood. It does not mean everything is predestined. We all have a free will. If we are not careful, we may not hear answered prayer or find the people we are to meet. We also have to be careful not to misinterpret providence, especially when we think of God's will. So often I have heard people say, "It's God's will," and then close their minds to any other considerations or directions. I believe we can only truly understand God's will, what he wants for our lives, in hindsight. We can never fully know it in the present or the future, only in the past. Is God's will, then, useless as an indication of where we are to go and what we are to do? No. We must be sensitive to the things happening around us. Cautiously, we say that we believe this is what God wants us to do, the best that we understand it. Then we proceed on faith, keeping our eyes open for possible course corrections. Providence, however, has to do with both the present and the future. Events occur, signs appear along the roadside, and people we need to know come along. God's will is what He wants us to do; providence gives us the provisions to do it.

Still, the skeptics shake their heads in disbelief and cast aspersions on the very idea of providence. To them, it all has to do with mathematic probability. You roll the dice enough times and your numbers will eventually come up.

Well, let's see how many super computers you'd need to calculate the mathematical odds of the following story. It definitely had divine providence written all over it. Take it from a skeptic who was reformed when confronted with so many such stories, I couldn't explain them all away.

From this . . .

To THIS! The Center for Humanitarian Aid and Disaster Relief. The American flag waves proudly next to the flags of the countries we serve.

Matthew 25: Ministries' Chairman of the Board, Michael Brandy.

Matthew 25: Ministries' Board Member David Knust.

First work party at our new facility. Front row (left to right): Rev. Mettey, two volunteers from First Christian Church of Harrison, staff member and all-around handyman John Marker, and Joe Elfers from the Church of Matthew 25. Second row (left to right): Mike Elam from the Church of Matthew 25, three additional volunteers from First Christian Church of Harrison, and staff member for local donation pickups Fred Hansberger.

The author's son, Tim Mettey (left), and a summer volunteer power wash a very dirty warehouse ceiling—five times!

During renovations, twenty-two forty-foot dumpsters of waste were removed from the building. John Canfield, M25M staff–inventory control, operates the forklift.

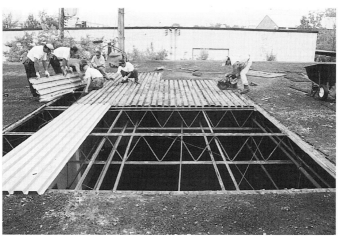

120,000 square feet (2.75 acres) of roof had to be repaired or completely replaced.

Cintas Corporation President and CEO Scott Farmer, a friend and advocate for Matthew 25, speaks at the Center's dedication ceremony October 3, 2004.

Cintas is a company with a heart for the needy. The Cintas Humanitarian Aid Processing Center, located in the Center for Humanitarian Relief, processes 750,000 pounds of supplies each month.

Director of Operations Patty Dilg, M25Ms' first staff person.

Joodi Archer, development and public relations, encouraging those assembled to purchase the author's first book, Are Not My People Worthy?

Volunteer and Processing Coordinator Anita Bowman. She gives a lot of TLC to volunteers.

Don and Paula Marcello, corporate donations and data entry.

Don Olson, chief financial officer. He quit his well-paying job to help the poor.

Dick Dostal, forklifting and warehousing. The best forklift operator east of the Rio Grande.

From a rusted-out pickup truck to a fleet of trucks.

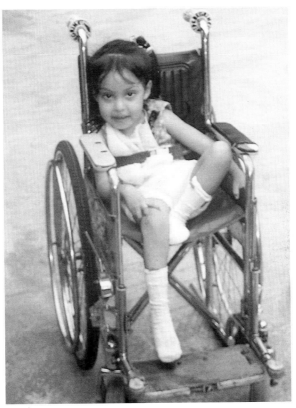

The miracle of the wheelchairs.

The Widow's Mite—two lepta coins.

Protecting the environment and saving lives. From our beginning through 2007, Matthew 25 has shipped more than 58,000,000 pounds of rescued and reused aid to those in need worldwide.

Tim Mettey (left) was Matthew 25's advance team of one. Traveling the affected region after Katrina, he determined when, where, and how much relief should be sent into the devastated area.

Her name was Katrina . . . the costliest and deadliest hurricane in the history of the United States.

For thirty-five consecutive days, Matthew 25 kept its doors open to receive and ship out supplies. During that time, 2,700 people volunteered at our facility.

The devastation of the tsunami was swift and deadly. The weak and helpless were its most numerous victims.

No real-estate agent . . . no "for sale" sign. . . . Within a few weeks, three people stopped in our Loveland facility to see if we wanted to sell our building and grounds.

June Keeling, an army of one. Volunteer extraordinaire, surrounded by a few of the more than 17,000 stuffed animals she collected for sick and poor children.

Children in Nicaragua are the happy recipients of some of June's stuffed animals.

At the back of this building is our first warehouse in 1990—just a mile from the building we eventually purchased—a seventeen-year journey back to where we started.

Site of warehouses 2, 3, and 4. No more rent-free warehouses.

Site of warehouses 5 and 6. This warehouse was built over a stream, with a roof which seemed to disappear during rainstorms.

Warehouse 7, "the old Ford plant." Freezing in the winter, sweltering in the summer.

Warehouse 8. Our biggest and most expensive.

A typical day of trucks coming and going at the Center for Humanitarian Relief. More than one thousand trucks come and go each year.

As the sign proclaims, Matthew 25: Ministries is truly a "doorway to helping the needy of the world."

Chapter Nine

Let the Little (Special Needs) Children Come Unto Me

We were traveling in the northern part of Nicaragua, about a four-hour drive from Managua. I had heard that there was a pastor in the area who was doing wonderful work with severely disabled children. Caring for a disabled child demands a lot of time, love, and patience. Caring for a disabled child in a poor country demands more than most families can possibly give. Severely disabled infants were often abandoned at his center, or left on the doorsteps of his home. No child was ever turned away. The name of this place translated literally was, "The Little Blue Bird Home."

In my travels, I have seen many such places. They were overpopulated, understaffed, and poorly financed. They were always a depressing sight. Some of my most seasoned fellow travelers would no longer go into these places. Seeing children in such deplorable conditions was more than they could bear.

After asking directions from what seemed to be every person in the entire village, we almost turned around and went back to Managua. Finally, we turned a corner and there it was. We had arrived at a freshly painted building with a mural of blue birds on the building's exterior. We were immediately greeted and escorted into the solarium, where we waited for the pastor. From where we were standing, we could see a portion of the courtyard. Children were everywhere, affected with every conceivable crippling deformity.

The pastor arrived and gave us a warm welcome. He was very excited. He heard of Matthew 25: Ministries and our work in Nicaragua. He took us on a tour. The odor that was always present in the other facilities we visited was thankfully missing in this one. In those facilities, children were left in bed all day, only receiving attention or touched when they were fed or their diaper was changed. Their clothes were changed only a few times each week. I don't want to give the impression that the workers were purposefully neglecting the children. There simply was not enough staff or resources to do more.

We could see immediately that this place was different. Each day the children were bathed, fed, dressed in clean clothes, and taken to the courtyard, weather permitting. There they were constrained in high-back chairs. Most sat under a large mesh tent which protected them from insects. As we passed, they smiled. Their heads turned from side to side, their arms flailed in all directions. When we touched them, they roared with laughter and made sounds acknowledging our presence.

Every bed was made daily. Diapers were changed when needed, and the infants were held as much as was possible. The ceramic tile floors were scrubbed throughout the day, and the chairs were old but neatly patched and disinfected routinely. No child was permitted to stay in bed unless he or she was taking a nap or sick, no matter how busy the staff. The rooms wore the signs of age, but were brightly painted. The roof didn't leak, and there were curtains on every window. There was a nice breeze circulating throughout the entire facility.

I was simply amazed and delighted to see the loving care these children were receiving. I asked the pastor about this and he quoted a passage of Scripture, "When you do it to the least of these you do it unto me." He had convinced every member of his staff that when they cared for these children, they were caring for their Savior who bled and died for them. He asked me if I was familiar with that Scripture. I just smiled.

As we concluded our visit, the pastor pulled me aside and thanked me for coming. I thanked him for the quality of care he was giving to the children. Characteristic of the Nicaraguans I have met, he wanted to ask for something, but hesitated. He did not want to appear to be ungrateful. I took the lead and asked him if there was something he wanted me to send him. No sooner had my words cleared my lips when he said, "Wheelchairs! The children need specialized wheelchairs," he pleaded. Many of the children had to be tied to chairs not designed for such use. If they had wheelchairs with head and neck supports, the children could be more mobile. The special chairs would help greatly with their physical therapy. Not wanting to give any false hope, I said that in the years I had been doing Matthew 25: Ministries, I had never seen such a wheelchair come into the warehouse, but I told him I would do my best.

The day after I returned from Nicaragua, I went to the warehouse physically tired and mentally exhausted. Patty Dilg, our first staff member who eventually became the director of operations for Matthew 25: Ministries, was already there. She told me that there was a truck at our dock, and the driver was asleep in the cab. Banging on the door of the cab, we awakened the driver. He said he had a load of "stuff" for us, that is, if we were Matthew 25: Ministries, which we assured him we were. He had no invoice or bill of lading. He did not know where the load came from, and he had no clue what he was hauling. All he did know was that he wanted to find a home for it and then find a place where he could sleep.

Great! we thought. The two of us would have to offload this unscheduled load. We opened our dock door, and then the door of the truck. Once it was fully opened, I just stood there in disbelief. There before my eyes was a truck full of children's wheelchairs, complete with accessories and attachments. The Scripture that came to me when we opened the truck and saw its contents was, "Jesus said, 'Let the little children come to me, and do not hinder them, for the kingdom of heaven belongs to such as these'" (Matt. 19:14).

No one will ever convince me that this was anything but divine providence. God had made provisions for these disabled children long before we even knew about them. Did God use a magic wand? No, he used people with free will— people who allowed God to use them to bring about this miracle. Someone along the way talked to me or Patty about wheelchairs. Then that person spoke to someone else, and there the wheelchairs were at our dock door. This providence business is all about showing up, being available, and patiently waiting for God's perfect timing. On that day, God said, "Here are the wheelchairs I want you to send to the children in the place called The Little Blue Bird Home."

Oops, I was wrong. This *was* a scheduled delivery.

Chapter Ten

The Ugly Duckling: Could This Be the One?

The following words appear in the Board of Directors of Matthew 25: Ministries minutes for September 29, 2003:

> Pastor Mettey reported that we are currently spending $22,000 each month on our Loveland mortgage and Highland lease payment. The Highland property is our ninth warehouse [we've occupied] in twelve years. Dave and Michael have been looking with Pastor Mettey at properties that fit our criteria; central location for volunteers, convenient for truck and car traffic, can house both warehouse and office staff at one location. We have found a facility in Blue Ash on Kenwood Road [11060 Kenwood Road]. Seven acres, 132,000 square feet . . . the asking price is

> $2.5 million. We have offered one million
> dollars and $600,000 as a tax write-off
> [with a high enough appraisal value]. It will
> cost $600,000 to repair.

It was time to fish or cut bait. We had toured the Kenwood Road building and property owned by the Keco Company four times, and said "Thanks, but no thanks" four times. It needed to be given a proper burial more than it needed a new tenant. Yet something kept bringing us back. In the past year, we had made a citywide tour for potential warehouses. A few I would have taken in a heartbeat, some I became quite desirous of, and I thought for certain this or that one would be the one. But something would always happen that killed the deal.

It was after another exhausting, disappointing day of warehouse shopping that Michael, Dave, and I came back to my study in Loveland. We tried to cheer ourselves up, but to no avail. Breaking the silence, Dave said, "You know, maybe we should go through the Keco building again. We haven't been there since we wrote it off three months ago. I'm certain most of Keco's stuff has been removed, which will give us a better look at space possibilities." From the real estate side, Michael said that it had been just sitting there for two years with little interest.

Of all the buildings we looked at, this was the dirtiest and the one with the most structural and renovation concerns. If it had any promise, it was difficult to see. It reminded me of the signs posted around the city, "We buy ugly houses." Well, this was the ugly warehouse.

A quick drive around the parking lot and a walk through the building made it quite evident that this place was never the recipient of any TLC. The offices had not been used for ten years. The carpet reeked of mold and mildew. Few of the light switches worked, and those that did had to be turned off and on at the electrical panel boxes. The leaky roof welcomed in the rain, which poured into the offices, down the walls, and onto the carpet. Black mold blossomed everywhere. The drop-ceiling panels were either missing, discolored, or ready to fall on someone's head. Nothing had been painted since paint was invented. Most of the commodes were turned off, and the others would overflow when flushed. Many of the sink faucets were heavily corroded and could not be turned on or off.

The warehouse itself was dark and dingy. Flickering fluorescent lights dangled from the rafters and came in all shapes and sizes. Most of them were in the last throes of electrical death. The roof of the warehouse was as porous as a kitchen colander. After a rain, water gathered in large puddles on the filthy concrete floor. A maintenance worker was quite ingenious when it came to dealing with one large leak. First, he placed a fifty-five gallon drum on the floor. He then got a ladder long enough to reach the ceiling located directly over a pod of makeshift offices. He next took a plastic sheet and tied one end around the lead in the ceiling and ran the rest of the plastic down into the drum below. When it rained, water ran down the plastic into the drum. When we saw it, the drum was half full of rain water and sported an abundance of green algae floating on the surface.

Everything in the place had immediate needs. The docks needed major repairs, the heating and air-conditioning system needed to be replaced, the walls and ceilings needed to be spray-washed and painted, most of the roof needed to be removed, twelve offices on the warehouse side needed to be demolished, thousands of feet of wiring needed to be traced and taken out, outside drain pipes needed to be repaired and unclogged, the large asphalt parking lot and trucking area needed to be coated, the outside of the building needed to be painted, the grounds needed major landscaping, and the entryway needed considerable renovation.

The cost of all of this? Dave said a ballpark estimate would be $600,000. Gulp!

The Keco building had two redeeming qualities that were on our "must have" list—location and size. The facilities and land were located on Kenwood Road in the city of Blue Ash. Kenwood Road was a main artery of the city; thousands of vehicles traveled it every day. During the day, the population of Blue Ash rose from twenty thousand to more than seventy thousand as workers from all over Cincinnati drove into this business-friendly industrial park encompassing more than two thousand businesses.

In 1961, Blue Ash became incorporated as a Charter City and its leaders went about the task of carefully blending both its commercial and residential, making it one of the most livable and "workable" cities in Ohio. The city's name came from a group of Baptists who settled there between 1797–1828. They built their church building out of the abundant blue ash trees growing in the area.

The size of the building was also a plus. From the road, it seemed much smaller. I had driven by it numerous times, but even when the large "for sale" sign went up, I thought it was just too small for our operation. Once inside, however, we were greeted with a 120,000-square-foot warehouse divided into three large bays. The largest warehouse we had occupied previously was 80,000 square feet. It had a huge parking lot and a 16,000-square-foot side lot that could be used for outside storage or possible expansion.

The building's history and activities of its owners are filled with innovation, economic boom and bust, and criminal activities.

In the early 1920s, Paul H. Davey developed the revolutionary Davey Compressor, (the first lightweight, aluminum, portable, air-cooled compressor) which contributed to a logging industry boom. In 1929, the Davey Compressor Company became incorporated. In the 1960s, the family sold the business. In 1974, its new owners moved the company from Kent, Ohio, to the location we were considering. Between 1977 and 1980, a cafeteria was added and the warehouse and dock areas were expanded to accommodate growth and house over two hundred employees. During this time, the company became a U.S. Defense Department contractor. Then, on October 7, 1983, following a long investigation, the Davey Compressor Company pled guilty to twenty-five felony counts for overbilling the government almost two million dollars. New management drove the company into bankruptcy in 1986. It was then purchased by the Keco Company.

When the Keco Company moved into a larger facility, a large "for sale" sign was put up and stayed up for two years, again, as Michael said, "with little interest." He said he had one nibble and a few walk-throughs when the sign first went up, since then—nothing. So far the interest had been in the land. People were not thinking "fixer upper," they were thinking "tearer downer—builder upper."

Our realtor friend, Bill Keefer, said that the listing price was $2.2 million, but because of the dire condition of the building and grounds, he thought the price could be greatly reduced.

It was Christmas 2003. We decided to make a bid. I was off to Nicaragua, Michael would put together an attractive offer, and Dave would take a closer look into what it would cost to renovate.

Chapter Eleven

Let the Negotiating Begin

As a 501(c)(3) federally recognized not-for-profit, we had an advantage over other for-profit businesses that might want to purchase the property. For example, if the building was given an appraised price of $2.5 million, we could offer the owner one million dollars cash and the owner could then take a tax write-off of $1.5 million. And that is exactly what we tried to do. This is where it gets rather tricky and complicated. First, the building had to be appraised (valued) by an un-biased, outside, professional appraiser. The appraiser, when arriving at a value for the building, looks at what similar buildings in the area are selling for. These are called comparables or "comps." Next, the appraiser takes into consideration the condition of the building. Let's say the Keco Building was appraised at $1.5 million. We could still offer $1 million cash, but the tax write-off for the owner could be no more than half of that.

There is also something else which complicates the cash/write-off proposal. Using the same example, the owner may not receive all of the tax benefit of the half-million dollars, but only up to a certain limit in the year the building was sold. The maximum charitable donation cannot exceed 10 percent of the company's net income in that year, but can carry over any unused amount. The owner can take the write-off in any of the next five years until fully utilized. Since we didn't know the company's financial position, we couldn't determine if such a deal was worth it to the company.

While the details were complicated, there was nothing complicated about the response to our bid—dead silence. Either our proposal was just brushed aside and deemed unworthy of consideration, or the bidding game had begun. Finally, we learned that our first proposal of $1 million cash and $1.5 million donation would not work. Both of us knew that the $2.2 million asking price was too high. So, on January 9, 2004, we flipped the numbers. We offered $1.5 million cash with a potential $1 million char-itable write-off. They countered on January 15 with a proposal of $1,750,000 cash and $5,000 earnest money. Bill notified us that there was another bidder, so we raised our bid $5,000 to $1,755,000. Keco also wanted their clean-up cost not to exceed $50,000.

Clean-up cost was certainly an issue. Throughout bay three, there were welding stations. Black dust was every-where. There were also large dipping vats inside and outside which had to be removed. A huge, metal painting booth needed to be cut up with torches and hauled away. Environmental concerns were ever-present. The age of the building and its former uses could have created a minefield of asbestos and lead paint. Removal and disposal of contaminated items could greatly exceed the $50,000.

Our thirty-day inspection period expired. To stay in the game, we had to ante up an additional $45,000 earnest money.

All this time, Michael was negotiating the sale of the Loveland building. He would have preferred working with only one prospective buyer at a time, but the good Lord sent us three. Then, one church dropped out. It was now down to a small church, which could have financing issues; and a business that was ready to go. Michael turned his attention toward the business and was moving rapidly to closing when a few neighbors raised objections to the intended use of the building.

We did not know what use the prospective buyers had in mind for the building. We only asked that the building would not be used for anything that would reflect poorly on Matthew 25: Ministries, such as an adult bookstore. We were assured it would not, but there was no way we could control its use once sold. A few days later, we learned that the building was going to be converted into a firing range. The firing range idea received the backing of the police, and handgun and rifle groups who needed firing ranges for their officers and members to practice the proper use of firearms. The new owner of the range was willing to go to extraordinary lengths and expensive measures to alleviate the fears and concerns of the neighbors. The entire matter ended up at city hall, where the neighbors won the first round of what turned out to be a protracted zoning battle.

Michael called me when he heard the news. The closing, which was scheduled in a few weeks, looked dead in the water. But, unbelievably, the owner still wanted to close on the building and property; the consensus was that they would eventually win the zoning battle. A few weeks later, we closed on the sale of Loveland building that we had built with our own hands. The irony is that the business won the zoning case, but the firing range never materialized. The building is now a pet store.

Chapter Twelve

The Widow's Mite

T hings were getting serious. Michael was working on closing the Loveland facility. He was also talking with the bank and working out the details. Dave and I were practically living at the Keco Building, trying to get a handle on all that needed to be done. The "need to do" list grew longer and longer. Until we started pulling up the old roof, we wouldn't know the extent of the needed repairs. I had a lot of confidence that Dave would give us the best cost estimate of what needed to be done. One item that concerned us was the unknowns regarding the environmental clean up. To our advantage, Michael and Dave knew a lot of individuals who could quickly come and estimate the cost of rehabbing the building and getting the finances needed.

In early March, the three of us met in my study to compare notes. The bank was willing to finance the project, but had a number of stipulations. Someone would have to personally guarantee $350,000 of the loan. The same amount from the proceeds of the capital campaign could only be used for the renovation work. The rest had to go toward the mortgage. We could understand the bank's position. We had no savings and only two months of operating reserves. We had just begun the task of putting together a campaign committee. The only thing of value we possessed was the equity in the Loveland building and property. We also had a great credit history.

Dave's news wasn't any better. The roof needed major repair and the heating and air-conditioning had to be completely replaced. The list went on and on to the tune of about six to seven hundred thousand dollars. And there was something else, potentially a deal breaker. One of our biggest concerns was the cost of utilities. Every time we toured the building in the winter, it was so hot we had to take our coats off. We knew we could do a better job of keeping the heating costs down. Before we met, Dave discovered the utilities were surprisingly low. The company was paying out approximately $6,000 a month. We could live with that, especially if we installed a new HVAC system, and only heated and air conditioned the areas of the building on an "as needed" basis.

At the meeting, however, Dave said that there was something more. He slumped back in his chair and said that he had only been given the electric portion of the bill. When he got the heating portion, the cost jumped from $6,000 to $17,000 per month. Along with all the uncertainties of renovation costs, he said, "My advice as a businessman is not to buy the Keco Building." We just sat in total silence. We took a deep breath and decided to sleep on this latest news.

The day before this meeting, I'd had a phone conversation with a member of my church, Gail Dean. Gail and her husband, Bob, had only been members of the church for a short period when Bob died of a brain tumor. He was a former FBI agent, and simply put, a beautiful human being. All during his fight with cancer he wrote a daily prayer list, a habit he had formed since becoming a Christian. Each morning, he'd update his list and then literally pray for everyone by name and need. He did that faithfully until his last few days.

Gail was now a widow and was faced with many decisions. Should she sell her house? Should she move closer to her aging parents? Since Bob took care of the finances, she was now faced with making many financial decisions she hadn't made before. She sold her home so she could better care for her parents. She went back to college to finish her degree. She became friends with a woman from Nigeria who was raising money to dig wells so the village of her birth could have clean, germ-free water. The two traveled to Nigeria and celebrated the successful drilling of their first well. Gail always impressed me with her depth of character, many talents, and spiritual sensitivities.

She picked up on the sound my voice that all was not going well with our efforts to purchase the Keco building. She asked about the progress. "The HVAC system alone, Gail, is going to cost us $80,000!" "Oh," she said, "That's a lot of money!" She called me back the next day. She said she had been thinking about our conversation, and after much prayer and going over her finances, she wanted to give—I thought I heard her say—$8,000. I thanked her for the offer, but said so much was still needed. . . . She interrupted me and said, "No, Wendell, not $8,000—*$80,000*. That's what you said the HVAC system would cost, didn't you?" I was silent for a moment, then managed to repeat, "Yes, I said $80,000." As her pastor, I was concerned for her financial situation as a widow. She said that Bob didn't leave her a million-aire, but she had enough. Then she said simply, "My needs are very small."

When we hung up, I thought of the story of the widow's mite. One day, Jesus was at the great temple in Jerusalem. He had been debating with the religious leaders and was looking for a quiet place to meditate and rest. He found such a place in what was called the "court of the woman" (Mark 12:41–44).

There were actually three temples built on this site. King Solomon built the first temple in seven years. (It took him fourteen years to build his palace). This temple was burned by orders of King Nebuchadnezzar of Babylon. The Persian king, Cyrus II, captured Babylon and laid waste to the Babylonian Empire. He also stopped the deportation of the Israelites and allowed many to return to Jerusalem for the rebuilding of the temple. Lacking in money and skilled craftsmen, the second temple was built by Zerubbabel. The returning exiles completed the temple on the third day in the month of Adar 515 BC (Ezra 6:15). While many referred to this temple as "substandard," it stood for 495 years. For religious and political reasons, King Herod, who reigned when Jesus was born, rebuilt the Zerubbabel temple. It was burned by the Roman Emperor Titus some thirty years after Jesus' death. Its ruins are the ones we see in modern-day Jerusalem. The Herod temple is where we find Jesus in this Scripture.

The Temple was a concentric series of courts. At center was the Holy of Holies. Only the high priest could enter this sacred space once a year on the Day of Atonement. The next court was the court of the priests, followed by the court of Israel, then the court of the women, and the last was the court of the Gentiles. The court of the women was the court where people made their offering. Offerings were placed in the thirteen collection boxes which resembled horns—narrow at the top and bell shaped at the bottom.

Jesus watched the people make their offerings and couldn't help but notice how a few made theirs. They first attracted attention to themselves by making exaggerated movements, using scripted gestures. With their heads piously bowed, they made certain everyone saw that they put their offering into all thirteen collection boxes. Oohs and aahs were heard throughout the courtyard. They were center stage, the main event. Who could love God more or be more righteous?

Amidst all of this piousity and ostentatious display, Jesus' eyes fell upon a widow quietly trying to make her offering, greatly ashamed, no doubt, by the worth of hers compared to the offerings of those who had just given so much. If her offering was small, her status in the community was even smaller. A popular prayer in her day went something like this, "Oh God, I thank you that I am not a criminal, a Gentile, or a woman." Women, unless married, or widowed with independent wealth, had little power or social status in the community. But Jesus would have nothing to do with gender ranking or class divisions. In God's eyes, all people were of equal worth; but their gifts were not. The people in that courtyard would say that the larger gifts were of greater value, but Jesus said the widow's gift was of greater worth because of the circumstance in which it was given.

The widow's offering was two lepta. It was the smallest of the coins, and translated it meant "the thin one." It was the equivalent of one-twentieth of a U.S. penny. It was also called a "mite." In Jesus' eyes, this poor widow gave the largest gift. It had the greatest value because of the sacrifice she made in giving it. The others gave out of their abundance; she gave out of her poverty. She didn't do it for the show; she did it because of her love of God. Perhaps that week she received a small blessing, or maybe she was remembering with thanksgiving the life of a deceased loved one, possibly her husband or a child. So great was her love of God and faith in Him that she gave not one, but two mites. Today, when someone gives sacrificially we call it "the widow's mite."

I saw Gail's gift as a message from God to continue with our plans to purchase the Keco building. I knew we could not fail because the very first gift toward it was sacrificially given. God was speaking through Gail's gift, reminding me that Matthew 25: Ministries had always been a faith journey. We had received a green light from God, and although there would still be many trials and tribulations to be experienced and obstacles to overcome, God was ahead of us, waving us on. He had made this provision long before we had gotten to this point in our journey.

I called up Don, Patty, Michael, and Dave. They were taken back by such a generous gift given under such circumstances. I told them that I was convinced that we could not fail. In less than twenty-four hours, the dream we thought was dead had new life, and we had renewed determination.

We became participants in that ancient story and knew our work would be blessed by the sacrificial gift of the widow's mite.

Chapter Thirteen

A Daily Reminder

S eldom does a day go by that I am not reminded of the children I have seen in my travels. Their smiling faces are a source of great joy, their little diseased bodies a cause of deep sadness. All we had done and were continuing to do was for them. I didn't need to go to Nicaragua or some other poor nation; all I had to do was open the newspaper, as I did that morning.

I unfolded the morning paper and placed it next to my bowl of cereal that teemed with fresh fruit. It was supposed to be a quiet breakfast and a few moments with the morning news, a check on the weather, a few headline stories, a comic or two, and then off to work. Instead, I found myself unable to take my eyes off of the child in the photograph before me.

What horrible circumstances could have brought him to such a moment of despair? I wondered. Vivid memories of atrocities witnessed. Separation from his family—all dead, no doubt. Herded into some makeshift refugee camp surrounded by a sea of unfamiliar and equally frightened faces. Standing now in line for food, perhaps his first meal in days, he places his little hand to his face, prematurely aged by nightmarish worries. He breaks down and cries. At that moment, the hellish realities of his world became more than he could bear.

Rwanda or Nicaragua; dark skin or light; curly or straight hair, it makes no difference, does it? They are the children of the Third World caught up in a grown-up world gone so terribly wrong. Abandoned. Orphaned. Malnourished. Diseased. Uneducated. Their photographs will never be lovingly placed in a family album. They are the ones we see in the newspapers or on the evening news. Their pictures are not taken in a studio against a backdrop of a variety of idyllic scenes, but standing crying in some food line or dying in their mother's arms. And yet, they differ from our children only in where and when they were born. We whisper quietly, "There, but for the grace of God, goes my child. . . . "

Staring at this little boy, I thought, *I have seen this child before*. I saw him running from car to car in a busy dangerous Nicaraguan intersection. For a dime, he'd wash our windshields so he could buy some food for himself and his little naked sister, whom he was carrying. I saw him in a little girl peeping from the doorway of a mud hut on a dusty road going to a poor Nicaraguan village: dirty faced, wearing only ragged panties, large hollow eyes, swollen stomach, chewing on a discarded piece of sugar cane. I also saw him lying in a Managua hospital, terribly dehydrated from diarrhea, his mother wiping his face with a damp rag. That evening, the family carried him home wrapped forever in a sheet.

I cut out the photograph of the little Rwandan boy. I simply could not bring myself to throw it away. I did not want him to endure one more indignity, no matter how small or unnoticed. It has become for me a daily reminder that this little boy's tragic story is being lived out daily by millions of children throughout the world. I cannot allow my easy life to remove me even farther than the physical miles that already separate us. I have to resist the temptation of getting so caught up in my world that I forget those who suffer so in the Third World. And if this photograph helps me do that, then this little boy's tragic life will have a purpose his world would deny him.

What do you feel when you see this child? I desperately want to take him in my arms and assure him everything will be all right. Sadly, I know I cannot. I pray to God daily that someone does. I can, however, take into my arms the children I *do* meet in life and the countless children through Matthew 25: Ministries! While the result of our work is in God's hands, the effort is in ours. Our new warehouse would become a beacon of hope to children and the poor who suffer so.

Chapter Fourteen

Be Careful What You Pray For

At the time, we felt like worlds were colliding, but in hindsight I can now see that everything was coming together as we had hoped for, as God had planned.

Each day brought new revelations about the extent of the needed repairs. In projecting the final cost of rehabbing the facility, we always took the worst-case scenario, and guess what? Almost every estimate we got back from the subcontractors was the worst-case scenario. It cannot be overstated; the building and grounds had been sorely neglected for years. With firm costs in hand, Dave made a strong case for lowering the price. We requested that the sale price be lowered from $1,755,000 to $1,605,000. The owner agreed! We now had $50,000 earnest money invested and a very dark cloud on the horizon, the environmental study scheduled for the end of the month. Dave believed the environmental issues were restricted to a certain area and would not be that expensive. Michael had successfully dealt with other properties that had environ-mental concerns. Unless there was something we had missed, it was a go. We put our hands to the plow and were not looking back.

We arranged for the closing to be pushed back to the end of April, just in case we had missed something.

We were fortunate when it came to asbestos; there was none. We were not as fortunate with lead paint. While confined to the 3,000-square-foot room at the southwest area of the warehouse, it took three men two weeks to remove the lead paint which completely covered the room.

We received a commitment to finance from the bank. Michael personally guaranteed a large portion of the loan until 60 percent of the loan was paid off.

We planned to move both our shipping operation from Highland to the Keco building when our lease expired in June and our offices from Loveland to the Keco building in early August. This would give us only a few months to get the Keco building ready to receive both facets of our operation.

Someone once said, "Be careful what you pray for, you just might get it." And did we ever!

The board of directors of Matthew 25: Ministries met on the evening of May 2, 2004. Motions were made to approve the sale of the Loveland building and grounds; to purchase the Keco property and building for $1,600,000; to borrow $1,850,000 from the bank ($250,000 for repairing the roof and installing a new HVAC system); and to create a Capital Fund Campaign to raise $2,500,000. All motions were moved, seconded, and unanimously approved.

On May 3, 2004, we closed on the Keco building. We finally had a home of our own, a warehouse worthy of the "least of these." It did not look like much, but it was ours, or should I say, God's. Buying such an ugly duckling was who we were. We would take products others would reject, work our magic, and send them to the needy of the world. We were not a glamorous operation, with the best equipment, working in the finest surroundings. We were successful and growing because we worked hard and were willing to make whatever sacrifice necessary in order to reach the poorest of the poor.

We did not get the keys to a building ready to do business, with nicely carpeted offices, a dozen docks that always opened with a push of a button, shiny warehouse floors, and freshly painted walls. Nor did we get a building with only a few items on the need-to-fix list. We got a warehouse that had Matthew 25: Ministries written all over it. God had chosen us long ago to be in the resurrection business. Our task was to take things that were old and make them new, to take things that were dead (or at least on life support) and bring them back to life. The temptation to have nicer things was always there. I was not seeking to live a sacrificial life without comforts, but I believed that our call to help the poor must be reflected both in how we conducted business and in our lifestyle. Not only was Matthew 25: Ministries called to care for the poor, but to speak to what has been called the monster of more, our insatiable desire as Americans to always want more things. Matthew 25: Ministries was not calling us to sell all we had and give to the poor, but rather to examine our lives and realize that if we live with a little less and give a little more, we could affect the lives of countless people who make up those grim statistics we discussed in the beginning of the book. We simply do not need all that we want.

Matthew 25: Ministries was also a place where writing a check and making a financial donation were greatly needed, but giving of oneself was of even greater value. When I would see entire families in the warehouse sorting clothes, pairing shoes, and inventorying medical supplies, I thought about the tangible lessons that those families, especially the children, will take with them for the rest of their lives. The sign says over the doorway at our processing center says it best: "Because you came today, someone will be helped tomorrow."

Chapter Fifteen

2004

I ronically, our twelve-year journey took us from the first warehouse we occupied in 1991, in and out of warehouses throughout the city, and finally back to a warehouse located just a mile away from the first one. It would have been much easier if God had walked us that mile and said, "Here it is, go for it." But as I already have said, as with the children of Israel, we were not ready then; now we were.

The Saturday after we closed on the Keco building, our first demolition crew arrived, twenty-five strong. Hammers, prybars, and saws in hand, we tackled the first of many sweat equity projects, dismantling ten substandard offices in bay one. We quickly discovered that we could not appreciate the horrible condition of the building by taking walking tours. The true condition of our new home could only be known when we started using our hands.

Instead of using existing wires or conduit, the previous owners just dropped new ones. Of the 109 fluorescent lights in bay one, only a handful of them worked. They were replaced with lighting fixtures that Dave bought off eBay, and with the help of my son Tim Mettey, they were assembled and installed. Tim also began living at the building. Before installing the lights, he pressure washed the entire first bay ceiling and walls three times. Each time, an inch or so of sludge was left on the floor, which had to be squeegeed down a very slow-flowing drain. Bay one would be our processing area, the place where our faithful volunteers would work. We wanted it to be as comfortable and inviting as possible. A generous gift enabled us to have it professionally painted.

The entrance foyer was remodeled and all the mold-laden carpet in the office area was replaced. Tim painted bays two and three. The overgrown shrubs and trees filled four forty-foot dumpsters. They were all shredded and used as mulch. New landscaping was added in the spring. The exterior of the building was painted blue and white. Flag poles were installed, and the American flag waved proudly over the flags of the countries we served.

Every day, a new discovery was made by our roofer, which usually meant additional cost. We finally came to the section of the ceiling we feared the most. This section was completely covered with a layer of rust. We suspected that the entire roof in that area would have to be replaced. It did, but included a larger area than we had anticipated. Halfway through the work, the roofers told us that they had run out of decking. Decking is best described as long pieces of corrugated metal which interlocks when laid side-by-side on the roof. Not only that, but their suppliers had run out, also. This would mean a two-to-three-week delay.

This was unacceptable. Our lease at Highland had expired and we needed to move our entire shipping operation to the Keco building within two weeks. There was no wiggle room.

Huddled inside the building discussing the problem, one of the roofers said, "Hey, what are you doing with those?" He was pointing to large corrugated panels that had been used as room dividers. We were going to sell them for scrap. The roofers said, "We can use them." They had enough decking to complete the job. To me, it was another small evidence of God's providential hand at work.

By the time we concluded the demolition phase, we had filled twenty-five forty-foot dumpsters with debris. All that we could salvage went to Nicaragua, and we recycled all we could. The larger jobs such as the HVAC system were wrapping up. But there were still hundreds of small jobs to do. Without Dave and Tim, we could never have completed all that we did in such a short time frame.

Incredibly, we were shipping and receiving supplies by the end of June, thanks to Anita Bowman, who headed up processing and volunteers; John Canfield and Dick Dostal, who ran the forklifts; and an increasing number of volunteers. The processing area was clean, freshly painted, and well lit. In August, our Loveland headquarters were moved to our new building, thanks to Patty Dilg, Don and Paula Marcello, Joodi Archer, Don Olson, and Fred Hansberger. We had also moved forward with our campaign committee and hired a campaign director. We were well into the campaign when it became apparent that the campaign director was not going to work out. A plan had been developed and literature printed, and now we had no one to guide and oversee the campaign. There was no time to search for someone else, so we hired a part-time staff person with campaign experience and ran the campaign ourselves. Joodi and Don O. were a tremendous help during this time.

We had a successful capital campaign. We did not receive as much as we wanted, but again, we got what we needed. The biggest surprise came when I received a call from Scott Farmer, the president and CEO of the Cintas Corporation, who had become a huge supporter, both personally and corporately, of Matthew 25: Ministries. The Cintas Foundation and Farmer Family Foundation together wished to give a sizeable grant toward our capital fund campaign. I was simply speechless. When I hung up the phone, I thanked God for Scott and Cintas and for the part they were playing in caring for the poorest of the poor. I didn't remember what I said to him, but hoped it conveyed how grateful we were. He said a portion of the gift would be paid out over a three-year period. When he told me that, I thought, *Wouldn't it be great if we could pay this warehouse off in three years?*

Chapter Sixteen

The Center for Humanitarian Aid and Disaster Relief

In our years of working with corporations and the public, one issue has become less of a concern but still sticks its head up from time to time. We are a Christian organization, a faith-based ministry. It is true that I, a Baptist pastor, founded Matthew 25:Ministries and that the focus of our effort and our very name comes from a passage in the New Testament. And while the motivation for our work grows out of a love of God and, therefore, a love for our fellow human beings, we do what we do because we have been instructed by Jesus Christ to care for the poor and needy.

I saw a sign recently that read, "Witness every day and if necessary you may use words." To me, the best witness of who we are is the work we do. Our work is to literally fulfill Matthew 25:34–40 by providing the basic necessities of life to the poorest of the poor: water, food, clothing, homes, medical and prison care.

One woman came by the office one day and said, "I am not of your faith but I believe in what you are doing," and gave a donation to our receptionist. I have always envisioned a place where people of all faiths and walks of life could come and work together toward a common cause and purpose. We are all human beings with the same needs. Surely most can agree that helping a needy child is something that could bring us together.

While we were in the midst of our capital campaign and rehabbing the new Matthew 25: Ministries' warehouse and headquarters, a name for our building came to me—The Center for Humanitarian Relief. These are the words I wrote during the campaign:

> In a world so divided, I have dreamed of a place where differences can be put aside and people of all faiths can work together toward the common, noble objective of helping a child in need. With the opening of the Center for Humanitarian Relief, this dream can become a reality. . . . The Center for Humanitarian Relief will serve as a dynamic processing and distribution center for our worldwide network of humanitarian relief. The Center's goal is to be an inclusive gathering place for people of all walks of life who wish to help those in need . . . the Center will continue to help those in need regardless of race, religion, or political persuasion.

We all felt an urgency to make the Center operational as quickly as possible. We pushed ourselves as hard as possible to meet the very ambitious schedule we had set. At times I'd think, *What's the rush? So bay three isn't ready. We can operate out of the processing center and bay two. No one's going anywhere.* Yet I kept pushing. I was obsessed with getting the entire building operational. It was hard to explain at the time; now, looking back, it is so clear. The name God gave me for our new building was not the Center for Humanitarian Relief. The prophetic name given me had actually been shortened by our capital campaign director, who said it was too long. The name that came to me was The Center for Humanitarian Aid and Disaster Relief.

We ship humanitarian aid to countries that are, you might say, in a perpetual state of needing disaster relief. The only real disaster relief we took part in was Hurricane Mitch in 1998. We didn't see ourselves in the disaster relief business, but in the ongoing business of humanitarian aid shipments.

That was soon to change.

Chapter Seventeen

Christmas 2004: The Tsunami

We were celebrating our first Christmas in our new home. A lot had been accomplished and a lot still needed to be done. We were operational, praise the Lord. The Cintas Humanitarian Relief Processing Center was running at full capacity. Bay two was filled with processed supplies ready to be shipped. Bay three sat empty, ready to be leased or for whatever the Lord had in mind. It was difficult to believe all that had been accomplished in such a short period of time. Since May, we had worked feverishly to get our operation completely up and running. Why? I wasn't certain. No one had an inkling of what we would face in the months ahead.

The day after Christmas we heard reports of a tidal wave hitting the coast of Southeast Asia. The initial reports were sketchy, but that evening we began seeing video images taken by tourists and hearing eyewitness accounts of the tidal wave, now being called a tsunami.

Tsunami comes from the Japanese of *tsu* (harbor) and *nami* (wave). Tsunamis are caused by earthquakes or volcanic eruptions deep in the ocean and can travel thousands of miles at the speed of sound. By December 27, it became evident that this tsunami would be catastrophic both in terms of property damage and the loss of life. While it traveled ashore only a few hundred yards, it hit the heavily populated coastal areas of eighteen countries bordering the Indian Ocean.

The earthquake that caused the tsunami was the second largest ever recorded, at 9.3 on the Richter scale, second only to the Chilean earthquake of May 22, 1960, which measured 9.5. The quake was felt from Sumatra to India. From December 26 to January 1, eighty-four aftershocks measuring between 5 and 7 shook the devastated areas.

The tsunami came without warning. In the Pacific Ocean area there is a warning system, but none exists in areas around the Indian Ocean. In the eleven countries hardest hit, the death toll stood at 226,566 people, an underestimation because so many were swept out to sea. It is also estimated that 1.5 million people were left homeless. Tragically, the loss of life would have been less in countries further from the epicenter if there had been a warning system to alert them.

The news media descended on the Center for Humanitarian Aid and Disaster Relief. On one morning, we had three television stations doing live reports from our warehouse, all asking the same question, "What is Matthew 25: Ministries going to do?" We knew we were going to respond to the tragedy in some way, but how, when, and what I did not know. We didn't have partners or a network in this area of the world like we had during Hurricane Mitch in 1998.

In October of that year, we had been in Nicaragua. While we were traveling though the country, Mitch was just a tropical storm lazily drifting around the Western Caribbean Sea. By the time we arrived at the airport to fly home, Mitch had strengthened to a Category Five hurricane. We were on the last plane heading north out of Nicaragua.

Mitch displaced the 1900 Galveston hurricane as the deadliest Atlantic hurricane. Nearly eleven thousand people were killed, and thousands were made homeless. Slow-moving Mitch dumped five feet of rain on Honduras and Nicaragua, causing massive flooding and mudslides that buried entire villages, killing everything. In Honduras, Mitch destroyed 70 percent of the crops, at a cost of one billion dollars. An estimated 70–80 percent of the transportation and infrastructure were wiped out, including all the bridges. Thirty-three thousand houses were destroyed and fifty thousand severely damaged.

While Mitch never officially landed in Nicaragua, the devastation was just as great. The villages of El Provenir and Rolando Rodriguez, which we had driven by on several occasions, were covered completely by a wall of mud when the side of the Casitas volcano gave way, killing more than two thousand villagers. Likewise, at least four other villages were completely submerged under seven feet of mud. Small monuments are the only reminder that this mud plain was once a village. Now it is a cemetery.

Hurricane Mitch was our first large-scale attempt at disaster relief. Within days, we were able to have relief supplies on the ground both in Nicaragua and Honduras because we were well-established in these countries. We had already developed a network for receiving and rapidly distributing supplies.

But six years later, how were we going to respond to the tsunami disaster? We moved as quickly as possible to locate partners that already had a system of distributing aid in the affected countries and that could quickly expand their operation without being overwhelmed. Within weeks, we had established contact with highly recommended part-ners and began making arrangements regarding the items needed and the seaports we would be using.

We immediately received a donation from the Cintas Corporation of 150,000 new articles of clothing, which filled six forty-foot containers. We already had in the warehouse much of the supplies needed, and other products came pouring in: hospital and first-aid supplies, food, cleaning products, and personal care items. In total, we shipped sixteen forty-foot seagoing containers filled with disaster relief supplies; the shipment weighed 362,010 pounds and was valued at $6,084,672. Early in January, friends of Matthew 25: Ministries representing many faiths gathered at the Center for a candlelight vigil. I said these words:

> People have varying levels of disposable income, but everyone can give of their time to remember and pray for those in such desperate need and who have lost every-thing. People need to feel that they can reach out and help in whatever way is best for them and we welcome that help.

Children have come with sandwich bags filled with the savings from their piggy banks, articles of clothing, and with cards of concern. During such times, people have a need to come together and be with other human beings; light a candle, say a prayer, and in their hearts remember other human beings who are hurting terribly. While miles and language and, sadly, religion may separate us . . . we are all human beings. This is what Matthew 25: Ministries is all about . . . helping human beings help other human beings in time of need.

Reflecting on that time, I could now see why we were in such a rush to become operational. God was getting us ready for the tsunami. What we did as a disaster relief effort was miniscule compared to what the world's governments, international corporations, and large not-for-profits did, but we played a part and began thinking of ourselves as a disaster relief ministry. In less than six months, we would be called upon in a way we never quite imagined. It was then we truly would become the Center for Humanitarian Aid and Disaster Relief.

Chapter Eighteen

Her Name Was Katrina: 2005

We were settling in. Except for the roof, most of the major repairs were completed. From January 1 to August 31, we shipped out 202 containers, weighing 4,142,369 pounds with a fair market value of $26,192,886. In the United States, we shipped supplies to the American Indians in South Dakota and Arizona, and to Appalachia and Greater Cincinnati. We were also expanding our reach overseas. During those eight months, we shipped supplies to Guatemala, Jamaica, Nicaragua, Grenada, Guyana, St. Lucia, Haiti, El Salvador, Sierra Leone, Trinidad, Jordan, Belize, and the Dominican Republic.

Toward the end of August, the Cintas Humanitarian Relief Processing Center was flooded with supplies ready to be processed, and bay two was completely full. Our small, full-time staff and a growing number of volunteers simply could not keep up. We came up with the idea of having part-time flexible schedules for stay-at-home moms. They could work around their family schedules, and still provide us with more people power.

Bay three still sat empty with no nibbles on the "for lease" sign posted in front of the Center. I did have restrictions on who I'd lease it to. Dave and Michael kept kidding me about having big eyes and really not wanting to lease it, thinking we'd grow into it. It was like the line in the movie *Field of Dreams*: If you build it, they will come. This was partly true, especially when you looked at the growth numbers we had already posted for 2005. There was also another reason. I had a feeling that it was a special, even sacred, space. It resembled the Tent of Meeting, or the tabernacle, that the Israelites took with them during their forty-year wilderness journey. It was a place where God and man came together. I believed that something special was going to take place and that room would play a large role.

Then it happened.

Monday, August 29, 2005, a hurricane named Katrina bullied her way into the Gulf Coast and cut a path of destruction as far north as Jackson, Mississippi. In New Orleans, the storm's heavy rainfall caused the levees to break, putting 80 percent of the city underwater. It would be the nation's most costly natural disaster. The statistics were staggering: More than 1,600 people were killed; 200,000 homes were destroyed; one million insurance claims were filed; and the estimated dollar damage was $25.3 billion. Within one year after the storm, the federal government would send $110 billion into the area.

The day after Katrina hit, a few people dropped off supplies they had purchased at the supermarket. The news media began calling and asking us how we were going to help. More and more people dropped off supplies and asked if they could volunteer. Soon the drop-off lines were ten to fifteen vehicles deep. News reports began showing the devastation, which prompted more donations and volunteers. Fifty, seventy-five, and soon one hundred people came each day to help. We cleared off the dock, divided the area, and strung signs overhead: cleaning products area, personal care area, adult food and baby food areas, first-aid supplies, and water. We assigned some people to off-load, others to sort, and still others to palletize and plastic wrap the pallets and forklift them into bay three.

Sorting supplies was crucial. When they reached their destination, they needed to be ready for immediate distribution. Also, you don't want your truck to be held up and unable to be off-loaded on the other end. That's why all of our supplies were on pallets, allowing our truckers to be off-loaded in about one hour. I cringe each time I see well-meaning people fill trucks with unsorted supplies crammed into those black trash bags. Never, never, *never* send disaster relief supplies that are not sorted! The people on the other end do not have the facilities or manpower to handle unsorted supplies. Also, in the United States, the last thing disaster areas want are clothes. Unsorted clothes shipped into disaster-stricken areas can create significant environmental concerns. Unable to sort and distribute unneeded clothing, relief workers have no choice but to throw them to the side. This happened during Katrina disaster relief. Huge, rain-soaked piles of black plastic bags dotted the landscape and were eventually hauled away to the landfill.

Our organization was in the disaster relief mode again. Bay three was rapidly filling up. The situation on the coast was deteriorating. The response by Matthew 25: Ministries and other organizations was heartwarming and historic. This was not some faraway country, but right here in America. These were not people who dressed differently and spoke a foreign language. They looked like us and spoke like us. They were fellow Americans; many were family members and friends. Many of us had lived, visited, or vacationed there. Katrina did not distinguish between race, religion, age, or economic status; anything in her path was destroyed. People saw the pictures on the news and wanted to help as they never had before. It was not like the tsunami, when many sent in a cash donation. This time, people wanted to help with their own hands and give of their time. They wanted to take their children to the store to buy food, diapers, or a case of water and bring what they purchased to Matthew 25: Ministries and say to them, "Do you remember those people we saw last night on TV? This is going to help them." And then they stayed.

I decided to treat this as I would a Third World disaster. We had an epicenter of destruction, and people were fleeing to major urban areas, needing immediate help. On September 4, we sent an advance team headed up by my son, Tim, into the devastated area to find the people and organizations doing the best job of receiving and distributing relief supplies. We established person-to-person communications and developed relationships with partners there, eliminating red tape. Tim made repeated trips into the area. We shipped only what was asked for—and when it was needed. Through telecommunications, we tracked every load we sent. We prayed and relied upon God for direction.

We put the word out that we needed truckers. We paid for the gas, and they began hauling our supplies. First, it was to the northern edge of the destruction in Jackson, Mississippi. Initially, there was a real concern that the truckers would not be able to find gas for their return trip if they went as far as New Orleans. We were thankful that never happened. Soon, we began paying the truckers on a per-mile basis, but when the government doubled the going rate, we had difficulty competing. In the end, however, whenever we needed something shipped, we found a trucker. We heard that the truckers loved hauling for us because of the quick turnaround time. Some truckers hauling for other organizations got stuck for days with full loads because there was no one to off-load them. The people in the impacted area looked forward to getting our products, which were top quality, carefully sorted, and exactly what they asked for.

We kept the Center for Humanitarian Aid and Disaster Relief open for thirty-five consecutive twelve-to-fifteen-hour days. In the month of September, we had 2,400 volunteers. It turned out to be the most active hurricane season in recorded American history (twenty-seven hurricanes in all). During the last four months of 2005, we shipped ninety semi-tractor-trailer loads carrying 2,370,416 pounds of disaster relief to hurricane victims. One month alone, we shipped fifty-two semis carrying 1.5 million pounds. All in all, we shipped a total of 137 semis carrying 3,542,580 pounds, with a large percentage of the supplies coming from ordinary citizens who responded during all of the activity to the extraordinary need.

One day, during all of the activity, I stood for a few moments in the dock area and thanked God for what I saw. More than eighty volunteers were feverishly unloading vehicles, carrying products to designated areas, plastic-wrapping pallets of supplies, and forklifting pallets of aid into waiting semis. The volunteers were as diverse as any group can be: young, old, African American, Caucasian, Jews, Muslims, and Christians, all working as one. All differences were put aside; they were simply human beings helping fellow human beings in a time of need.

Chapter Nineteen

The Year Isn't Over Yet

While we were busy responding to the mess Katrina left behind, Central America and Mexico were also feeling the fury of hurricanes and tropical depressions. Hurricane Stan was the eleventh Atlantic hurricane of 2005. It was a relatively weak storm; however, it dumped torrential rains in Central America, hitting El Salvador and Mexico particularly hard. Stan and the huge weather system that spawned it caused an estimated 1,620 deaths. Many believed this to be a conservative number, however, as thousands more remained missing.

The call went out for disaster relief. Matthew 25: Ministries responded by sending supplies beginning on October 13, 2005. Somehow we had thirteen forty-foot containers of supplies already processed in our Center, and they were immediately shipped to El Salvador.

Just five days before we shipped our first container to El Salvador, the world awakened to the news that a major

earthquake had hit Pakistan. A month after the earthquake, the death toll was reported to be over seventy-three
thousand persons, mostly villagers who lived in the remote
mountains of northern Pakistan.

This opened an avenue to working with the Muslim
community in Greater Cincinnati. We had a number of
meetings and planning sessions primarily with those who
had connections to Pakistan. Along with providing logistical support for sending supplies collected by the Muslim
community, Matthew 25: Ministries shipped to Pakistan
twenty-two forty-foot containers of winter jackets, blan-
kets, medicine, food, medical supplies, etc. weighing
415,156 pounds and valued at $1,092,176.

Needless to say, 2005 was a record year for Matthew 25:
Ministries. It was also a year that took a toll on me both
physically and emotionally. I found myself developing
insomnia. During the height of the Katrina relief effort, I'd
waken at two or three o'clock in the morning, unable to go
back to sleep. I worried that we would not have the strength
or the level of commitment that was needed to continue
receiving and shipping truckload after truckload each day.

The year 2005 was certainly a defining moment for
Matthew 25: Ministries and the Center for Humanitarian
Aid and Disaster Relief. When we closed down for the
Christmas holidays, the totals for the year were amazing.
From Christmas 2004 to Christmas 2005, we shipped 417
containers/semi-tractor trailers weighing 8,933,481 pounds
with a fair market value of $54,071,454. It was only then
that I realized why we had pushed so hard to get the
Center fully operational and why bay three was not leased.
Once again, we were participants in God's providential
plans. When we needed it, His provision was there.

Chapter Twenty

A Little Oil

Compared to her situation, the proverbial rock and a hard place would feel like a feather bed. In her time, a woman could not be in a worse predicament. She lived in the days of the great Old Testament prophets. Her husband had died, leaving her enough IOU slips to wallpaper her home. Her husband was a good man, but times were hard and his profession didn't pay much. He was a member of the company of prophets, as they were known. He served God in one of the holy and famous cities of Bethel, Gilgal, or perhaps Jericho. The great prophet Elijah had recently died, creating a leadership vacuum. Politically and economically, the entire region was in upheaval. The only way her husband could supplement his income was by incurring debt. We have no reason to believe that he was irresponsible. He simply did not think he'd die when he did. Neither did his wife.

Now his creditor stood at her door, demanding satisfaction of her newly acquired debt. The only items she possessed that had any economic value were her two sons. Under Mosaic Law, her sons could be taken to pay off her husband's considerable debt. Such servitude was a common practice. Without her sons to take care of her, she'd never see old age. She would surely die of deprivation, or of a broken heart.

While her gender and finances were against her, she was not powerless. As with so many of the women in the Bible who faced similar situations, the power she had and used so effectively was tenacity. In this case, driven by the love of a mother for her children, she went looking for the prophet Elisha, who had picked up the mantel Elijah laid down. Before she asked for help, she told him that her husband also had served as a prophet. He served Elisha, and possibly Elijah, in this company of prophets. "Your servant my husband is dead, and you know that he revered the Lord. But now his creditor is coming to take my two boys as his slaves" (2 Kings 4:1). She subtly implied that being a prophet demanded much sacrifice, not only from the prophet, but from the entire family. His job hardly paid enough to keep food on the table. She and her husband didn't complain then, nor was she complaining now, but he was dead and the creditor was knocking on her door.

An interesting dialogue between the prophet and the widow ensued. He asked her two questions: "How can I help you? Tell me, what do you have in your house?" (2 Kings 4:2). She said she had nothing except a little oil.

Oh, how God loves that answer, "a little." A *little* yeast works through the whole batch of dough (1 Cor. 5:6), a *little* faith moves a mountain (Matt. 17:20), a *little* boy's lunch feeds the multitude (John 6:9), a *little* shepherd boy defeats the giant (1 Sam. 17:49), a *little* seed becomes a great tree (Matt. 13:32), a *little* light shines brightest in the darkness (Matt. 5:15).

Elisha seized on this not only to solve her problem, but to teach her, and us, an important lesson. The solution to her problem had to do with the size of her faith. He told her to gather up all the vessels she could find or borrow from her neighbors and take them to her house, away from the prophet, so she would know it wasn't him but God doing these things. Behind closed doors, she started pouring her "little oil" into one vessel after another. The oil did not stop flowing until the last vessel was filled. She still had the original jar and her little bit of oil in it. The woman was able to pay off her husband's debts. She and her sons lived happily ever after.

From the time we first began to consider purchasing the Center for Humanitarian Aid and Disaster Relief, we always tried to think of some revenue stream that would help us meet, or perhaps even pay off, our mortgage. We were taking on a huge debt, and we didn't want the creditor knocking on our door. We had considered leasing bay three. It was the largest of the three bays and could generate some needed revenue. Compared to the

Highland warehouse, our new facility looked gigantic. We thought it would take at least two to three years of growth before we'd need it.

We had a parade of people come through with all types of needs and requirements. From the start, I was not comfortable with the idea. I really could not say why, but I didn't want to turn down revenue that we could count on to help pay down the debt we had incurred. Within a short period of time, we had gone from having a few months of operating funds, no savings, and perhaps $500,000 equity in the Loveland building to incurring a $2.2 million debt.

Yet bay three sat empty. On a few occasions, a large donation of supplies would find its way there, but quickly it emptied. Then Katrina came calling. Within a matter of one month, the 2,400 volunteers who showed up to help and the carload after carload and truckload after truckload of supplies that poured in, filled and emptied bay three *more than twenty times* during that period. To this day, bay three has never been even close to being empty.

It was our lesson of faith, our vessel of oil. We could never empty our Center for Humanitarian Aid and Disaster Relief or, for that matter, any warehouse we've occupied. As with the widow, the amount of the donated products we received was in direct proportion to the size of our facility and the speed in which we could ship it to the poorest of the poor.

Chapter Twenty-One

On Kairos Time

The Ancient Greeks had two distinct words for time. The most common word was *chronos*. It expressed the duration or length of a period. This is where we get the English word "chronology." The other Greek word was *kairos*. It was used to describe the special features that occurred during that period. In short, *chronos* meant quantity of time, whereas *kairos* meant the quality of time.

We have little control of *chronos* time. We are all born, and we all will die. We have no say about when we are born. The health choices we make in life can lengthen or shorten our lives. However, the words of Ecclesiastes are correct. There is "a time to be born and a time to die" (Eccl. 3:2). While we have little to say regarding *chronos* time, we have complete say as to how we are going to use it. *Chronos* is the time we are given; *kairos* is how we use that time. And when we are on *kairos* time, wonderful events happen that live in our memories for the rest of our lives. We might be fuzzy on the actual *chronos* time, that is, when it happened and in what sequence, but we will always remember the *kairos* time event.

So it was with the thirty-five months from May 2004 to March 2007. While I had to do a great deal of research for this book to get the *chronos* time correct, I had no difficulty at all remembering the *kairos* experiences—the wonderful, hard to believe, incredible, meaningful time that it was and will forever remain in my heart and mind. But I'm getting ahead of myself. Here's what happened and why those thirty-five months are still difficult to believe.

After we sold the Loveland building and completed the capital fund campaign, we had cash donations and pledges to pay down the mortgage and pay for all of the $600,000 repair and renovation work. Interest rates were still low, so we took the risky path of paying only the going interest rate. We hoped to pay down the principal on the loan as money became available. Interest rates were inching up, so we knew we couldn't stay on this path very long. We considered having another capital campaign in three years, when the pledging period was over. That was not the way I wanted to go. Instead, I decided to do something different.

First, we would commit ourselves to paying off the mortgage, even if it meant reducing the shipment of supplies and cutting back on operations and some of our programs. I had many long conversations with God about the possibility of sending less to the poor. We had purchased our own facility to keep us from putting so much energy into moving around and to rid ourselves of high lease payments. If we did not focus on debt reduction, we were just trading lease payments for mortgage payments. I decided that a significant portion of undesignated money would go toward paying off the mortgage.

To accomplish this, Don Olson and I created an internal account labeled Mortgage Retirement and Reserve Fund (MRRF). Our previous monthly lease and mortgage payment was $22,000. Since we were only paying the interest on our present mortgage, our monthly payment was considerably less than that. I decided to take a portion of the savings and put it in this MRRF. Then, at the end of the year, I would decide what financial cushion (the undeflatable kind) we needed to go into a new year and put the remaining balance in the MRRF. This would be conditional on the giving, which for me was a sign that God approved of this plan.

The *chronos* time clock began in May 2004 and kept ticking through 2005, the year of the three monstrous catastrophes—the tsunami, Hurricane Katrina, and the Pakistan earthquake. During those periods, especially Katrina, hundreds of envelopes came daily, each carrying generous donations. 2005 became our single biggest giving year ever. Naturally, a large portion of the donations were designated for these disasters. As is our policy, 100 percent of designated donations goes to the designated cause.

I wondered if there would be any undesignated donations we could use for operations or put into the MRRF. People had given so generously to our disaster relief efforts, would most of their charitable budgets be used up for the year?

Almost unbelievably, we received an overflowing financial blessing from God's people. While we spent a considerable amount of money on these disasters, especially Katrina, we still had funds to put in our MRRF.

Thirty-five months after we purchased the Center, the following emails were exchanged:

From: Don Olson
Sent: 03/01/2007 11:20 AM
To: Matthew.Weis
Subject: Pay off of Matthew 25:
               Ministries mortgage

This morning I transferred $xxx,xxx from the Matthew 25: Ministries' investment account to the money market account. When the transfer is complete, please pay off the mortgage balance of approximately $xxx,xxx using funds from our money market account. Feel free to call me if you have any questions.

Thanks, Don Olson

From: Matthew Weis
Sent: 03/02/2007 09:02 AM
To: Glenda.Parrott
Subject: Fw: Pay off of Matthew 25:
               Ministries mortgage

Please pay off the note today as detailed below. I assume there will also be interest due and a $40 recording release fee. Please bring me the tickets to sign and confirm when done.

Thank you, Matt

From: Glenda.Parrott
Sent: Friday, March 02, 2007 11:32 AM
To: Don Olson
Cc: Matthew.Weis
Subject: Fw: Pay off of Matthew 25:
               Ministries mortgage

Just wanted to let you know we did verify the transfer of $xxx,xxx today into the money market account ending with xxxx. Per your request, I debited this account and process the following payoff for the C/L # ending xxxx.

$xxx,xxx
Principal $xx.xx
Interest $xx.xx
Recording Fee

Total debit to money market account is $xxx,xxx. If you have any questions please let me know.

Glenda

From:	Don Olson
Sent:	Friday, March 02, 2007 11:51 AM
To:	Wendell Mettey
Subject:	Fw: Pay off of Matthew 25: Ministries mortgage

It's paid off!!!!!

Don

In just thirty-five months, we paid off our debt of $2.2 million. Even the most optimistic among us did not think we could pay off the debt in such a short period of time. Equally amazing, we did not have to curb our shipments. Quite the opposite: we shipped a record number of containers.

Someday, we will remember those thirty-five months, and we will debate whether it was thirty-three or thirty-five months. We won't remember. That's the way it is with *chronos* time. But we will never forget the *kairos* time event. Something truly wonderful happened, and we were privileged to play a part in it. In reflection, it was longer than just thirty-five months. It began on that first trip to Nicaragua in January—or was that December? 1990 or 1991? It's not important. It's the experience that will stay with us, because we have been on *kairos* time.

Chapter Twenty-Two

Lessons Learned

People often ask me what lessons I have learned from my seventeen-year journey with Matthew 25: Ministries.

First, I have learned that I have not been on a journey, but on a pilgrimage. Often these words are used interchangeably. However, they are different when used in a spiritual context. A journey is more than, say, a trip; that is true. A journey implies a meaningful venture. It is a time of searching for whatever compelled us to begin our journey. We can journey by ourselves or with others, who we call sojourners. When we embark on a pilgrimage, the emphasis is not on getting there, but on what the pilgrimage does to the person. The person becomes a pilgrim, the very embodiment of the venture. Pilgrims search as do the sojourners, but a pilgrim's search is never over. The destination is the pilgrimage. The one on a journey travels to an end goal; the pilgrim is on a never-ending quest. One is elated at the finish, the other is transformed by the experience. Our journey has come to an end. We have accomplished what we set out to accomplish seventeen years ago. But it is not over. We are more than sojourners. We are pilgrims, seeking to know more about ourselves and the poor we serve. Even more important, we yearn to know more about the God who sent us on this pilgrimage.

Second, I have learned that God's timing is perfect. He is the God of yesterday, today, and tomorrow. He sees far in advance and works to bring all things together. We can remember yesterday and see only today. We cannot see into the future, nor do we know all the intricacies of God's plan—who He wants us to meet or those He wants to meet us. Our tendency is to rush ahead and then complain to God that things didn't work out as we planned. Well, I've learned it is not what Wendell plans, but what God has planned. I often tell people that when we get a big NO, it's because God has for us a bigger YES. We must do all we can and then trust that His will be done.

Third, I've learned that the title of the old gospel hymn is so true: "What a Friend We Have in Jesus." Jesus has been a fellow pilgrim. Jesus has been with us every step of the way, guiding, comforting, correcting, and encouraging. I've also learned what a friend the *poor* have in Jesus. Now, some seventeen years after my first visit to Nicaragua, I am still deeply bothered when I see children living in such filth and squalor. I can see Jesus with the poor, waving us on, saying, "Feed my sheep." Those who love Jesus express that love each time we tangibly help the "least of these," for when we do it to them, we do it unto Jesus.

Fourth, I have learned that if it is God's will, nothing is impossible. People often tell children they can do anything they want to do. This is poor advice. They can be anything God wants them to be. How do we know what that is? Simple: it's whatever you're gifted in, love to do, and have the passion for. Matthew 25: Ministries has been successful because we are people who have gifts in the areas of warehousing, soliciting, and finance, and we have a deep abiding passion to help the poor.

Fifth, I've learned to believe in miracles. I had seen so many miracle con artists in my thirty-five year pastorate that I became skeptical and concluded that real miracles only happened in New Testament times. Still somewhat dubious of claims of the miraculous, I have seen too many things happen that are unexplainable. I suppose you could say that the entire Matthew 25: Ministries story is miraculous. While we haven't raised anyone from the dead, we have fed a lot of hungry people and seen the sick and injured made well. Those are God's great miracles, those He works through people helping other people.

Lastly, the greatest lesson I've learned is: please, please remember, it is never what we desire. It is what God desires. Do you know what it's like to drive the streets of Cincinnati and say over and over again, "God, thank you that we did not get that warehouse, or that warehouse, or that warehouse. You know how I wanted that place . . . and that place . . . and that place . . . "

What we desire is so often less than what God desires for us. But remember that what God desires can come in the form of an ugly, ugly warehouse. Now, I know we could not have asked for a better warehouse or a more perfect location.

How do you know what God desires for you? I can only say, let your pilgrimage begin.